*f***P**

GAME
FRAME

Using Games
as a Strategy for Success

Aaron Dignan

FREE PRESS

New York   London   Toronto   Sydney

FREE PRESS
A Division of Simon & Schuster, Inc.
1230 Avenue of the Americas
New York, NY 10020

First Free Press hardcover edition March 2011

FREE PRESS and colophon are trademarks of Simon & Schuster, Inc.

For information about special discounts for bulk purchases,
please contact Simon & Schuster Special Sales at 1-866-506-1949
or business@simonandschuster.com

The Simon & Schuster Speakers Bureau can bring authors to your live event.
For more information or to book an event contact the Simon & Schuster Speakers
Bureau at 1-866-248-3049 or visit our website at www.simonspeakers.com.

DESIGNED BY ERICH HOBBING

Manufactured in the United States of America

1   3   5   7   9   10   8   6   4   2

Library of Congress Cataloging-in-Publication Data

Dignan, Aaron.
Game frame : using games as a strategy for success / by Aaron Dignan.
p. cm.
Includes bibliographical references.
1. Play—Psychological aspects. 2. Games—Psychological aspects. I. Title.
BF717.D55 2011
155—dc22
2010041683

ISBN 978-1-4516-1106-9

For Britt,
who challenges me in all the right ways

"We think big things drive big behaviors: if people don't go to school, we think they don't like school. Instead, most behaviors are driven by the moment."

—Sendhil Mullainathan

"You see, in every job that must be done, there is an element of fun. You find the fun, and snap! The job's a game."

—Mary Poppins

CONTENTS

BACKSTORY

The rules of the game were simple: sit quietly and calmly for one hour, receive a gift. Behave for another hour, get another gift. Through this series of rewards (or bribes, depending on your point of view) my parents got me through our annual cross-country drive to Ohio for the holidays.

Hourly bounty may not have been in the parental handbook, but I wasn't exactly your average kid. When I was just a few years old, my mother was filling a large moving box with craft supplies and found me sitting in it, staring into space. "Aaron, you cannot sit in there," she said sternly, and turned briefly away. When she turned back, there I was, *standing* in the box, with a defiant look on my face that said, *you'd better be more specific.*

They say necessity is the mother of invention. The drive from St. Louis, Missouri, to Mansfield, Ohio was eight hours long, and not particularly scenic. I was hyperactive, and had a reputation for being downright obnoxious if not properly occupied. So, my mother did what any good student of human behavior would do. She gamed me.

Before each trip, she would purchase and wrap a handful of new toys and prizes. Every hour of the drive was assigned a specific gift, and if I behaved myself during that hour, I got to open it. This give and take lasted the entire drive.

These prizes weren't expensive things—an action figure, a pack of baseball cards, or a puzzle were standard fare. Yet, they all had a few things in common: they were mysterious, fun, and connected to a system of rules that put me at odds with myself. I distinctly remember sitting in the backseat and squirming under the pressure of my own desire to misbehave, while at the same time feeling an intense curiosity about the next surprise to come.

In addition to keeping me relatively reserved, this little arrangement played some very interesting tricks on my sense of time. Rather than simply make the trip seem longer or shorter on the whole, something more complicated transpired. As I received each new prize, time flew by for fifteen minutes or so as I played with my winnings. Then, as the half hour mark neared, my thoughts started to turn to the next prize. Would it be better? Would it be different? Would it complement my current plaything? Time seemed to slow down. By ten minutes till the hour, I was a wreck—excited, jittery, veering out of control. And this dance continued, up to eight times over.

Did this make the trip seem shorter? Truthfully, it almost made the trip irrelevant. I was stuck in a feedback loop, and my thoughts were on the cycle of stuff, not the traffic signs passing by out the window.

Now, the economists reading along might say that my mother was simply baiting me with incentives—that this was an economic exercise. But the *experience itself* didn't feel quite that straightforward. For starters, the rules were ambiguous enough that I could stretch them. Good behavior, after all, is a loosely defined thing. It was up to me to push the limits, to find out where the boundaries were. And I did. That was the game—to wait out the hour by pushing my luck, pleading my case, and cashing in on what restraint I had. To my young mind, this was a *great* game.

Fast forward twenty years or so to the fall of 2008. Staring out the window of my New York apartment, I think to myself: I used to have fun. I remember playing in the sewers near my house thinking that exploring that network of tunnels was an expedition of epic proportions. One day I looked up and suddenly everything had become a bit boring.

I'm not alone. Many people I know feel that their job, their schoolwork, and even their free time leave something to be desired. We live in a world filled with many unsatisfying experiences. At the same time, games like the ones I played as a kid seem to have the power to captivate us and make us feel alive. I decided that I had to know why, so that I could make my life (and the lives of people around me) more compelling.

I started digging. As I learned more about games and play, it seemed as though the rest of the world was also waking up to their power. In business, many of the start-up success stories from the last few years owe some (or all) of their good fortune to games or game dynamics. Today, people are discussing the possibilities, and the debate around how and when to use games is a hot topic. My hope is to share some of the knowledge and power of game designers and game scholars with individual readers, like you, who want to be motivated—or motivate others—to achieve their potential, and have fun doing it.

This book is my attempt to compartmentalize the relevant information about games and play in everyday life into one quick but actionable read. The truth is, we are born knowing how to play, and how to invent games where none exist. *I'm convinced that there is a role for games and play in reshaping the world around us.* Most of the game designers I know imagine a world full of highly engaged people actively becoming the best version of themselves. In bringing that vision to life, we lack only the road map to get there, and the willingness to begin the journey.

Which brings me to my one disclaimer: I am not a game designer by trade, nor an academic in the field of game studies. I am a digital strategist and entrepreneur, and spend my days and nights exploring how digital technology has transformed culture (and will continue to do so) both around us and through us. In researching this book, I've developed immense respect for the academics whose work illuminates the power of games, designers and creative talents who make their living through them, and the psychologists and neuroscientists who continue to augment our understanding of the human mind at play. I was both challenged and inspired by their work in developing this material.

As we consider the future that we want to create and the

potential of games and play to help us get there, I think back to those long drives to Ohio. My mother, in her infinite wisdom, would surely remind us that if we work long enough and hard enough, and sit *very still* . . . there's a prize in it for us.

GAME
FRAME

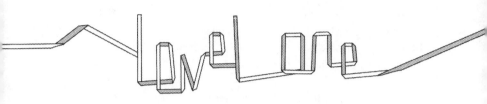

We're bored. Not all of us, and certainly not all the time, but it does happen a lot. Look into the eyes of the person behind the checkout counter the next time you buy something. Note the expression on the face of an employee in accounts payable who has held that same job for ten years. Observe a classroom of students during a middle school world studies class. Boredom is everywhere, and it's a by-product of poorly structured systems.

In so many communities and organizations, the lack of interesting and challenging opportunities is apparent. Teenagers with excess free time and hungry minds are forced to choose from a scant menu of options, often resorting to mindless forms of entertainment to pass the time. Adults in the workplace aren't much better off, but the demands of work and family life keep us busy enough to be complacent with the status quo.

Whether the fault lies with the systems that surround us or the way we're approaching them, boredom isn't the only thing holding us back. It's part of a larger trend of issues preventing us from realizing our potential. Some of us suffer from a lack of motivation. Others have problems with follow-through—eagerly starting new projects with verve only to lose steam over time. Still others feel helpless even to try, discouraged by the apparent difficulty of what lies ahead.

These feelings are all common among people who have

become disenchanted with "the system," whether that system is their company, their school, or even their personal life. Examining these issues and how they relate to each other, I've grouped them into two distinct symptoms: lack of *volition* and lack of *faculty*. By understanding how they inhibit us, we can attack them head on. Let's take a closer look.

> **Lack of Volition.** Volition is the *will* to do something; the motivation and internal drive to see it through. Any kind of proactive or ambitious behavior is evidence of strong volition. People who lack volition feel lost, bored, or disconnected from the task at hand. They can't see why an activity or behavior is worthwhile. A lack of volition is defined by disinterest, low involvement, and arrested development. An individual lacking volition says, "I'm not going to do that. Why would I? What's in it for me?"

> **Lack of Faculty.** Faculty is the belief that we have the skills and tools to handle the challenges we're facing; that we know how to begin and have the confidence to pursue our goals. People who lack faculty in a particular situation may feel that it's too hard, or that it's unclear what they need to do to succeed. A lack of faculty is defined by anxiety, submission, and ultimately, despair. An individual lacking faculty says, "I can't do this. I'm not prepared. I don't know how."

We can't bribe our way out of these issues. But that's exactly what we try to do. Faced with an unmotivated employee or student, our first instinct is to dangle a carrot (an incentive). If that doesn't work, we threaten him. In either case, we're missing the point. Tackling a lack of volition or faculty with blunt instruments like rewards and punishments simply ignores the fact that *the activities and experiences causing these symptoms aren't any fun.*

The Proof Is in the Pudding

Fortunately for us, one medium is designed to address these issues systemically: games. They do this through a structured and challenging system that makes the process of learning rewarding, enables deep engagement, provides a sense of autonomy, and asks us to be heroes in our own stories.

Games, in contrast to shallow rewards systems, are made up of activities that we genuinely like. They manage to pull us in and hold our attention almost effortlessly. This is no accident. Games are created with our enjoyment in mind. Josh Knowles, a software developer and designer, drives this point home on his website: "Games are engagement engines. To design a game is to take some thing—some basic enjoyable and/or satisfying interaction—and carefully apply rules to help players maximize the enjoyment and/or satisfaction they have with that interaction."

The point is that playing games is satisfying in and of itself. If we aim to overcome the lack of volition and faculty that we're facing, it follows that our experiences—be they at work, school, or at home—need to be enjoyable and satisfying in their own right. Layering a rewards system over an existing experience doesn't make us like it any better, it just encourages us to tolerate it.

And yet, game-like rewards systems have become quite popular. From loyalty cards to points systems to badges for achievement, organizations are beginning to see the value of game mechanics applied to everything from software to staff meetings. But while simply pasting game mechanics—the ingredients that make games work—onto an existing system is great for short-term engagement, it will almost certainly lead to diminishing returns down the road. The core experience of an activity matters, and a veneer of gameplay isn't going to change that.

If deeper engagement and performance are what we seek, we need to change our systems from the inside out. And in places where we can't, we must pay close attention to the way we apply a game layer to our lives. Because using play to influence behavior is more complicated than we think.

Learning Machines

Human beings are learning machines. Our brains are always hunting for patterns—exploring and experimenting—in order to increase our chance of survival. We learn in order to thrive, and it's our main method of interaction with the world around us. So it's not surprising that learning is often accompanied by enjoyment.

A game, at its core, is a kind of structured learning environment. In games, we learn two important things: new skills and new information. Game designers spend a lot of time thinking about skills in particular, because they are the basic framework of interaction with the game system itself. In the classic Nintendo game *Super Mario Bros.*, learning how to run and jump are skills that are fundamental to completing the game. Much of our engagement comes from the trial and error learning process of running and jumping with abandon, slowly turning clumsiness into precision. Once you've acquired those skills, you're able to move through subsequent levels far more freely. And of course, knowledge of each level—the location of every enemy and reward that lies in wait for you—is the other half of mastering the game.

That Learning Feeling

It's hard to tell *exactly* when we're learning. We have a sense that it's happening, but it's not a conscious process. We encounter something new, turn it over and over in our minds (or hands), and somehow, in the handling, it becomes our own. Mental connections are made, and we now possess something we didn't before. Along the way, while we're not aware of these connections being formed, we are aware of how we *feel* during this process. We feel riveted. We feel as if we're "getting it." We feel a sense of deep satisfaction.

To describe this process, game designer Raph Koster borrowed a wonderful term from the world of science fiction: grok. To grok something means to understand it so thoroughly that it becomes *a part of you.* Our brains love grokking new information, so we feel good when it happens. In fact, neuroscientists have shown that when we figure something out, our brains release a flood of chemicals known as opioids (nature's "pleasure drugs").

Any new skill or nugget of information represents a puzzle to our brains, one we feel compelled to solve. Once we grok it though—once it's understood—we need a new reason to stay engaged.

Funnily enough, the bored cashier at the checkout stand probably wasn't bored on her first day. She was swimming in a sea of new policies and processes, rules, and regulations. New behaviors and skills were required, and fast. She had a lot of things to figure out. But somewhere between day one and day thirty, she grokked the job. The pattern became clear, and her development slowed. Her boredom is a symptom of an exhausted system— one that is effectively saying, "Nothing else to learn here, just keep doing what you're doing." All that remains for her in terms of motivation is a nominal reward in the form of a weekly paycheck. That's simply not enough. As we'll see later, our volition depends on continued learning and growth.

Who's In Charge Here?

In games, we control the action by making our own decisions. Without our input, most games simply stop. This kind of autonomy is incredibly empowering stuff, and it's something sorely missing from the average person's day. Control represents both the freedom to act and interact with the system, as well as our ability to manipulate the world around us. In the game of basketball, the players each have control of their movements on the court, while they attempt to exert some measure of control on the ball itself. In most cases, the rules of play communicate to players what is and isn't under their control.

One of my favorite examples of autonomy in action is the Montessori method. Entrusted to educate a classroom full of five-year-olds, most of us would begin developing lesson plans.

With kids that young, structure is key—we need to manage their time and attention. Right?

Not necessarily. According to Maria Montessori, children have a natural way of interacting with the world around them that promotes learning and mastery. It's simple: put a group of kids in a room filled with creative supplies and resources, and get out of the way.

The Montessori method is predicated upon the belief (justified by years of experimental observation) that children are self-directed learners. At Montessori schools, students are free to explore whatever interests them, with the help of a teacher who acts as a guide. The sense of self-directed purpose they feel leads to a locus of internal control, greater engagement in the classroom, and rapid development.

Autonomy and control also play a role in creating a sense of self. We say to ourselves, "This is me, operating in the world, making things happen." When we participate in self-directed activities, we ascribe our own meaning and purpose to them, and can be certain that we're acting of our own volition. Our intentions are driving our behavior.

A lack of control in any system creates frustration. Nothing is more bothersome than knowing what to do and not being able (or trusted) to do it. In this way, the granting of control is a kind of validation—an admittance that a person is prepared to be "the hero." When we're making meaningful decisions, our sense of faculty and confidence is increased, and we're forced to think about our goals, which feeds volition.

Good Systems Create Flow

Our inherent attraction to games and the enjoyment they produce is a concept illuminated in Mihaly Csikszentmihalyi's *Flow*. According to him, human beings achieve a state of optimal experience when our skills are continually in balance with the challenges we face. This means that as we progress in any activity, we should be challenged just beyond the level of our abilities. This way, we have to grow ever so slightly to succeed. With each burst of growth, we reach ever higher for the next level.

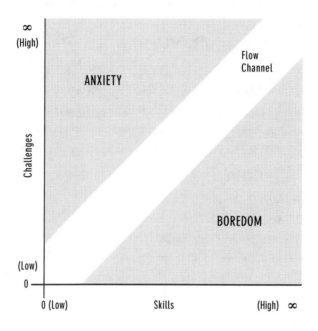

Flow activities induce a state of mind classified by enjoyment, loss of time perception, and a suspension of self. We've all experienced this at some point; perhaps it was during a big presentation at work, on a Jet Ski while on vacation, or while playing an intense video game with friends. We find ourselves so engaged, so in the experience, that we lose track of everything around us. Afterward, we feel an intense sense of exhilaration and accomplishment—a deep satisfaction with ourselves.

When described in these terms, you can begin to see how conducive to flow modern video games really are. Because they are immersive, engaging, and recognize achievement, they're a relatively common gateway into flow for people who are likely not feeling that sensation elsewhere. These games are literally giving players the best learning opportunities they can find.

Great games of all kinds do an excellent job of structuring the grokking process. They provide us with what we crave: a set of escalating challenges, feedback on our progress, and the thrill of victory. Systems lacking these elements almost always result in less enjoyable experiences.

With all that said, I don't believe that "the system" is solely to blame here. After all, some people do take low-challenge, low-control situations and turn them into wonderful experiences rich with engagement. You know how they do it? By playing the unlikely role of game designer. If they happen to work the checkout counter as a cashier, they make a game of how many people they can get to smile, or how many sales they can complete in an hour. Every day they try to beat their record, and on days when they do, they up the ante. They *create* a satisfying and escalating challenge instead of waiting for one to be given to them, and this approach literally changes their lives.

So my question is this: why can't everybody do this? Whether you call it creating flow or just plain playfulness, why is this skill set limited to a handful of gifted individuals and game designers? It doesn't have to be. The more we experience flow, the better we get at re-creating it. And each and every time, it reminds us how volition, faculty, and the challenge at hand combine to create balance.

Everyday Heroes

If you study our greatest myths and stories, you'll quickly find yourself discussing the hero's journey. It's a pattern in the plot of many of our most powerful stories and myths that was popularized by mythologist Joseph Campbell. A radical simplification of the hero's journey goes something like this: a "chosen" individual is called to higher purpose, is mentored by a wise elder, embarks on a quest, faces many trials, appears to perish but is reborn, confronts his nemesis, and emerges victorious. Sound familiar? It's a narrative structure that shows up everywhere: *The Count of Monte Cristo, Ender's Game, The Matrix*, and the story of Jesus Christ, to name a few.

One of the reasons that we love games is because they instantly place us on our own hero's journey, and from the comfort (and safety) of our living room. There's something tremendously satisfying about playing out an archetypal struggle in which each of us, for the duration of the game at least, is the chosen one. Unlike so many other settings where seemingly meaningless and repetitive tasks frustrate us, in games we are at one with our story. With the weight of the game world on our shoulders, we go about the business of saving the world from zombies, the princess from the evil sorcerer, our sports team from longtime rivals, or our fellow soldiers from enemy fire. Being part of a story, and one in which we know we're expected to prevail, plays to our sense of volition and faculty beautifully. We come to desire the victory that the story presupposes, and we simply *must* find a way to win.

I wholeheartedly believe that we can transform our everyday experiences into a billion heros' journeys, and that we can do so without an Xbox. To achieve that—to bring enjoyment to the most frustrating of circumstances (and democratize the process of creating flow), we'll need a whole new tool kit, and an understanding of games and play that goes far beyond pressing buttons.

What Lies Ahead

This book is divided into ten levels. With each turn of the page you'll progress toward a deeper understanding of games and play—ultimately learning how to design game-like experiences for yourself. Level One (which you've just completed) examined the issues of volition and faculty and suggested that games have lessons to teach us about realizing our potential. Level Two considers the rise of interactive technology and the state of games today. Level Three explores the somewhat misunderstood concept of play. Level Four offers a deeper look at games: how we define them, why we love them, and how they make us better. Level Five contemplates a possible future for games and the technology that will drive them. Level Six outlines the potential problems presented by a future filled with games. Level Seven reveals an altogether different breed of games that could reshape the world around us. Level Eight shares a methodology for designing those games. Level Nine profiles a handful of popular and applicable game mechanics and dynamics. Finally, Level Ten reminds us that the future of games lies not in preying on our compulsions but in realizing our potential. Enjoy.

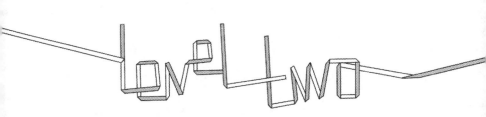

When I was a kid, the world had one button. It was bright orange and belonged to my neighbor's Atari 2600 Video Computer System. On the day he brought the system home we played until our fingers were numb. Later that night we paused, looked at each other, and sat in stunned silence. This thing was a revelation! What had happened to the past ten hours was unclear, but one thing was for sure: video games were for us.

It wasn't too long before video games began to show up in school. If you went to elementary school in the 1980s as I did, the line "You have died of dysentery" may hold a special place in your heart. It's from the now classic educational computer game *Oregon Trail*, in which a pioneer family travels west in covered wagons, trying to stay alive against the odds. *Oregon Trail* is but one of a deep catalog of video game staples that have touched the lives of millions over the past forty years.

The nostalgia I feel for *Oregon Trail* might kick in for *Where in the World Is Carmen Sandiego?*, *Math Blaster*, or *Prince of Persia* in your case. Or perhaps, *Ms. Pac-Man*, *Centipede*, or *Frogger* are closer to home. And of course, you can't leave out *Super Mario Brothers*, *Castle Wolfenstein*, *DOOM*, *7th Guest*, *Myst*, or *Golden Eye* either.

These games (and many many others) peppered an adolescence during which my entertainment options became infinitely

11

more intriguing. My formative years ushered in an unbelievable bounty of digital innovations, many of which had a profound impact on me. Here's a list *from memory* of the things I remember seeing along the way:

> Atari. Intellivision. Walkman. Game Boy. Macintosh. Casio digital watches. Nintendo Entertainment System. Apple IIGS. Sega Genesis. Neo Geo. Super Nintendo. TI-85 graphing calculator. Discman. PlayStation. The Internet. Nintendo 64. Palm Pilot. MP3s. Nokia 5110 mobile phone. Dreamcast. PlayStation 2. iPod. Google. Game Cube. TiVo. Xbox . . .

While those were wild times in their own right, the years since the introduction of the Xbox have packed more innovation than all previous years combined. As we look back, it's clear that literally billions of people have grown up in a world surrounded by accelerating technological change. The obvious question is: what has it done to us?

While there are many possible answers, I'll focus on just one: what this force of change did was provide us with a constant stream of new things to play with. These products provided real-time feedback and the opportunity to solve puzzles ranging from "How do I get to the next level of *Super Mario Brothers*?" to "How do I get this document to print?"

For early adopters like me, this pattern of befuddlement and the ensuing hunt for a solution was constant. It pumped up our play muscles, and preyed on our brain's desire for new skills and knowledge. Opportunities to explore had always existed, but before technology went mainstream they were fewer and farther between. This new world of games and gadgets had our number, and we were hooked.

Golden Age of Games

As games continue to evolve in the years ahead, I'd argue that we may be living in the *golden age* of games. That is, this may be the last moment when games are still relatively distinct from real life and the rest of our media landscape.

I say relatively distinct because clearly, the ground has already started to shift beneath our feet. If you played *Pac-Man* in 1975, you weren't thinking about a *Pac-Man* movie or comic book spin-off. You weren't reading about *Pac-Man* being acquired in the *Wall Street Journal*. Nor were you connecting with friends halfway across the world inside the maze of the game. And you certainly weren't accessing *Pac-Man* multiple times a day from your numerous mobile devices. You were just playing a video game, pure and simple. For better or worse, the days of pure and simple are numbered.

Blending In

As games and the technology that supports them continue to evolve, we're witnessing a trend of game-like experiences blending into our lives. What are American Express points, if not a game? Isn't *Guitar Hero* just a more engaging version of music lessons? And isn't Webkinz—a brand of stuffed animal that includes online access to a matching virtual pet—just the best of both worlds?

A location-based mobile application called Foursquare is another great example of the real world and the game world blending into one. The service applies game mechanics to the basic function of telling your friends where you are. Users simply "check in" to specific locations via their mobile phone when they go out, and those check-ins net them points, badges of honor for specific travel patterns, and (most important) real-world offers and incentives.

I would be remiss not to mention the trend of alternate reality games (ARGs) that have been increasingly popular in the last decade. At any given moment, there are dozens of ARGs happening around the world. One of my favorites, *Street Wars*, is a multi-city global event that asks participants to assassinate each other.

At the beginning of the game, players are provided with a manila folder that contains the name and address of another real live player in their home city. Their objective is to find and shoot this person (with a water gun or water balloon), before their own assailant finds and shoots them. You can scarcely imagine the ridiculous lengths that grown men and women will go to ensure victory in this game.

None of this is happening purely inside a screen. It's out in the living room, it's on the street, and it's in the boardroom. The time when games knew their place is long gone.

Seeing games as somehow distinct from everyday life is going to get harder and harder. Games are everywhere, and they're blurring the lines between play and reality.

The Business of Games

Arguably, the most powerful force driving the evolution of games is money. In *Joystick Nation*, J. C. Herz recounts that as far back as 1981, arcades around the country were collecting *20 billion quarters a year.* That's a $5 billion dollar gaming market that had to be made one coin at a time.

Games are an even bigger business today, and they're no longer trapped in the mall; they're everywhere. According to the NPD Group, a leading market analyst, total sales for the U.S. video game market in 2009 were $19.66 billion (about half of which was hardware). With total U.S. box office receipts coming in between $10 and $11 billion last year, it's clear that games are giving movie theaters a run for their money. Worldwide figures for the video game market are much higher, with some estimates hovering around $50 billion annually. PricewaterhouseCoopers estimates that the global video game market will hit $73.5 billion by 2013.

Individual game titles and systems routinely report astounding sales figures of their own. *Grand Theft Auto IV* is rumored to have grossed $500 million dollars in a single week. *Halo 3* has sold over 8 million copies on Xbox, and the *Call of Duty* franchise has sold an incredible 55 million copies across all titles and platforms. In the last few years, console systems like the Xbox, PS3, and Wii have brought gaming into the mainstream in a big way. Over 27.2 million units of the Wii console have been sold in the United States alone.

Clearly video games are a financial force to be reckoned with. But drawing conclusions about the size or shape of the industry is difficult at best, because so many new gaming platforms are cropping up every day. With all this growth, it's not surprising to see the demographics of console gaming change. According to a Sony report referenced in Byron Reeves and J. Leighton Read's book *Total Engagement*, the median age for a gamer today is thirty-three—only two years shy of the median age of the general population.

Of course, let's not forget that while *video games* are the subject du jour, games and play are broader concepts still. In examining the scale of gaming as an industry we can't ignore sports or gambling, two other manifestations that are colossal businesses in their own right. Combined as one force, games represent one of the most powerful and profitable areas of human experience.

Everybody's Playing

Video games aren't a fringe domain anymore. New offerings like *Wii Fit* are bringing a more diverse family audience to the category. And *FarmVille*, in which players manage the operation of a virtual farm, has millions of kids *and their parents* playing together on Facebook.

Rather than play in isolation, gamers have community now. Xbox LIVE is an extremely popular subscription that allows users to log on to a network of friends, on-demand content, and other tools. The service lets them play their favorite titles together with friends in multiple locations. With a headset microphone and real-time conversation, it's like being in the same room with your friends without ever leaving your couch.

Shorter, simpler, and more casual games have become

increasingly popular too. On sites like OMGPOP.com users can play games by themselves, or play live with people from around the world. The current juggernaut of this social gaming space is Zynga, the creator of *FarmVille*. The company built its early games on the Facebook platform, allowing hundreds of millions of people ready access to social gaming in the most obvious place of all—the world's most popular social network.

Traditional video game publishers are paying attention. In late 2009, Electronic Arts acquired social game developer Playfish for $300 million. Why? Because no one knows whether the next hit game will be played on a console, a social network . . . or both.

Other Worldly

One of the most widely discussed categories in gaming is the field of massively multiplayer online role-playing games, or MMORPGs for short (MMOs for shorter). These online games are social in nature, and create whole new forms of play and community. They connect tens of millions of people via never-ending fantasy worlds where players spend their time developing their avatar (character) by exploring the world and completing various types of quests and raids.

The most popular MMO, *World of Warcraft*, has approximately 12 million subscribers. While many popular games can be dismissed as fads, *World of Warcraft* membership has maintained a user base north of 10 million users for *three years*. With a subscription fee of approximately $15 per month, the business is generating roughly $180 million in revenue *every thirty days* with no end in sight. Beyond that, some estimates have pegged the aftermarket for characters and other items earned within MMOs at $1.8 billion.

Gamers treat the MMO space with a special kind of reverence. These worlds are not onetime episodes to be beaten and subsequently shelved. They are ongoing and evolving social worlds, complete with friends, enemies, jobs, rewards, and the passage of time. They don't stop evolving when you power down your computer. They live on. As a result, and in part because the gameplay of these worlds is so engaging, players invest months of their lives into building characters that represent different (and often better) versions of themselves.

This emotional investment is powerful. In one famously humorous and unsettling YouTube video, entitled *Greatest freak out ever*, a teenage boy discovers that his mother has terminated his *World of Warcraft* account, and with it his avatar. His violent and devastated reaction is almost indistinguishable from the grief you'd expect if he had learned of a death in the family. With MMOs, the emotional stakes are high.

The Demographic Shift

What's most intriguing about the social and casual gaming revolution is how dramatically it's changed our idea about the demographics of gamers. A recent study sponsored by PopCap gives us a view of the landscape in early 2010. Of the roughly 100 million social gamers out there, only 6 percent were twenty-one and younger. Women outnumbered men. Respondents reported an average age of forty-three. And 41 percent of them worked full-time. On average, they had been playing for more than a year, and many reported that their playtime was increasing, indicating habitual use. To put this in context with the overall population, look at it this way: at the time of the study, one in four U.S. and UK Internet users was playing social games at least once a week.

Our Games Reflect Us

In his classic *Man, Play and Games*, Roger Callois discusses the interdependence of games and culture. He believes that games reflect the culture that plays them, and that players are equally influenced by the games of the zeitgeist. If this is true, it sheds new light on our evaluation of the present.

According to this theory, games are becoming more diffuse,

more complex, and more social because *we* are. They are touching our lives in more places and more ways because we're ready for them to. And as the rest of our culture moves forward technologically, socially, and functionally, it's inevitable that our games will follow suit, and imprint on the next generation the very values we're creating today.

Gadgetry and Games

The explosive growth of the video gaming industry has driven plenty of competition and innovation, which is taking games in new and more integrated directions. Motion-based technologies like the Wii are becoming standard, prompting millions to interact with their game systems in a physical way. And while this may never replace traditional controller-based play, evolving technology is making it easier to interact with games.

The latest generation of these technologies comes in the form of Xbox's *Kinect* and PS3's *Move*. *Kinect* is an add-on device for the Xbox that uses sensors that allow gamers to play using their entire body. To punch the bad guy, just reach out your hand and punch. Playing a dance game? Dance. Meanwhile, *Move* is Sony's answer to the Wii, a new controller that offers sophisticated motion-controlled gameplay. Regardless of whether these innovations are good or bad (and there is much debate), they suggest that our future holds a more intuitive gaming experience.

One technology that is effortlessly bringing games into the real world is the mobile phone. The introduction of devices like the iPhone and the Droid has driven a whole economy of games in the form of downloadable apps that can be played anytime, anywhere, and in short bursts. Many of these games now upload data that feed online leaderboards, comparing your performance with players everywhere. Other games allow you to network several devices together to enjoy true multiplayer action. Some apps even allow users to view an additional layer of information and content associated with the physical world around them, a concept called "augmented reality." With literally hundreds of thousands of apps and hundreds of millions of smartphones in the wild, this is fertile territory for the future of gaming.

All of these innovations suggest a future with a much richer sensory game experience: one where you can move, see, touch, feel, hear, and perhaps even smell the action. This kind of immersion will continue to blur the lines between the real and virtual, making the effects of games even more potent and lasting.

Gaming Virtuosos

According to professor Luis von Ahn at Carnegie Mellon University, the average American born after 1970 or so will have played ten thousand hours of computer and video games by the time she reaches age twenty-one. Put another way, that's like 5.2 years of full-time work spent playing games. It's as if a whole generation—an entire crop of people woke up to find themselves at an Olympic training camp for gamers.

In her inspiring 2010 TED Talk, game scholar Jane McGonigal referred to this as a "parallel track of education" going on after (or even during) school. She believes, and I agree, that this phenomenon is creating "virtuosos" of game-based collaboration and problem solving. A generation of gaming virtuosos won't be content to play only in their spare time. They're going to look for careers that let them put those skills to use.

Playing for a Living

Until recently, being a pilot in the Air Force meant extended stays on foreign bases and significant flight risk with every mission. Today, a new crop of pilots are being trained to operate war drones, a class of unmanned aerial vehicles (UAVs) that are the future of warfare. Already deployed in record numbers in Iraq and Afghanistan, these remote-controlled spy aircraft are capable of high-resolution surveillance and targeted lethal force.

Coupled with their ability to remain above a target for twenty-four hours, and the fact that they can be piloted from right here in the United States, their popularity and demand far exceeds the number of pilots trained to handle them.

Luckily for the Air Force, millions of potential recruits have deep experience in interactive environments that mimic the drone interface. And though most of that experience has been logged on an Xbox 360 or Playstation 3, it'll do. To the Air Force, the countless hours that recruits have spent gaming is just preparation for their most recent job opening.

We'll see plenty more of this—employers putting gaming skills to use—in the years to come. Until then, gamers will continue to look for ways to play in their current jobs, however difficult that might be.

It's Good to Be a Gamer

Traditional employers should be trying to hire gamers too. Because if you stack up people who play games regularly against those that don't, some stark differences emerge. On average, which group do you think is healthier? Is closer with their families? Earns higher salaries? Is more socially connected? Has better visual skills and mental mapping? Has a faster cognitive response time? You guessed it, the regular gamers. In study after study, gamers come out ahead on a wide range of skills and abilities.

The challenging and rich experiences that make up most popular video games are literally rewiring gamers' brains as they play. And while some of these benefits take a long time to manifest, others can happen quite rapidly. One University of Rochester study showed that *just one week* of playing *Tetris* improved nongamers' visual recognition skills significantly.

Not only are skills improved in games, but attitudes and mental health are as well. Solitaire at work has been shown to improve morale. And a study reported by John Beck and Mitchell Wade in *The Kids Are Alright* demonstrated that young frequent gamers had a much stronger belief that things could be made better in the future.

Primed to Play

Several of my close friends have young children, and they've all told me how easily their kids were able to learn to operate an iPhone. I'm talking about two-year-old kids, adept at navigating the menus and functions of a touchscreen phone, opening apps they're familiar with, and using them. All this without much discussion or instruction, because in most cases, *these kids don't speak in full sentences yet.*

One of the things we know about the brain is that it is malleable—our wiring can change. Neuroscientists refer to this as neuroplasticity. According to them, individual connections within our brains are constantly being created, strengthened, or pruned, based on how they are used. Playing with games and technology every day of your life, then, is bound to have an effect on how your brain is wired. Whatever skills or cognitive processes are involved are likely to be strengthened. Which means that for anyone who spends a significant amount of time gaming, the way in which games communicate with players is something their brains are uniquely organized to perceive.

Several generations of grey matter are now primed to spot game mechanics. After ten thousand hours of play, and surrounded by technology, many of our brains are attuned to game-like stimuli as never before. If you think you're quick to spot a point system, or a puzzle, or a relationship between your behavior and a reward, just imagine what your kids will be capable of.

The Play State

The meteoric rise of video games has shown us a quite potent form of engagement. In living rooms across the country each night, packs of teenagers lie dumbstruck in the flickering glow of a flatscreen, mouths agape, eyes glazed over, their brains humming quietly. Their expression belies a common state of mind—a play state.

How that play state manifests in the brain, and why games possess such a magic hold over us, are mysteries we need to understand if we want to harness their power.

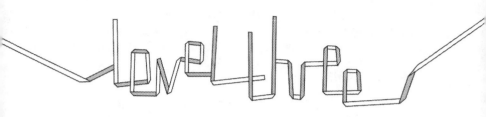

Want to feel good? Have a cupcake. That first bite will quickly trigger the release of opioids in the pleasure center of your brain. You'll feel a deep satisfaction and all will be right with the world, at least for a little while. This process is largely the same for many of our favorite rewards, including shopping, chocolate, and orgasms.

But what if you want to feel *motivated*? Well, that all depends on what you're trying to do. Video games, as you know by now, are remarkably good at encouraging people to do all kinds of things. Playing games, at least from your brain's perspective, seems like very important work indeed. This is not surprising, since a game usually comprises a series of little challenges and struggles, all designed to push you to the edge of your abilities, shift you into flow, and reward you when you succeed. But why is the structure of a game so attractive to your brain? What's really going on there?

To find out, let's quickly brush up on our neuroscience. The human brain is made up of a vast and dense network of special nerve cells called neurons. Neurons use electrical and chemical signals known as neurotransmitters to communicate with each other through junctions called synapses. Your brain contains approximately 80 to 100 billion neurons that are constantly communicating with each other by releasing and reclaiming these chemical signals. There are many different kinds of neurotransmitters in the brain, and they regulate a wide variety of processes, including those that regulate the motivation we feel while playing games.

What Drives Us

To truly understand the brain chemistry involved in gameplay (or cupcakes for that matter), we need to understand the neurological difference between *pleasure* and *desire*. From a neuroscientist's perspective, these are two very different things.

Kent Berridge of the University of Michigan is an expert in affective neuroscience and studies pleasure in the brain. He uses the terms *liking* and *wanting* to describe the processes behind pleasure and desire.

According to Berridge, there are certain hedonic hotspots located in a small part of the brain known as the nucleus accumbens. When we receive a reward, opioids and other brain chemicals are released to these hotspots and interact with the neurons there to, in Berridge's words, "generate a 'liking' reaction—a sort of pleasure gloss or varnish." Experiences that are pleasurable trigger this pleasure circuitry, which in turn tells us, "Hey, that really hits the spot." Liking, then, in Berridge's terms, is another word for pleasure.

Wanting, on the other hand, is primarily fueled by the neurotransmitter dopamine. Once thought to be the brain's primary pleasure drug, dopamine is now understood to be much more active in regulating desire and motivation. According to Steven Johnson in *Everything Bad Is Good for You*, "The dopamine system is a kind of accountant: keeping track of expected rewards, and sending off an alert—in the form of lowered dopamine levels—when those rewards don't arrive as promised."

When we don't find what we're looking for, lowered dopamine levels trigger that wanting sensation—and an invigorated search for the reward we're craving. Seeking, a concept originated by Washington State University neuroscientist Jaak Panksepp, is synonymous with wanting. Panksepp uses the term to describe an emotional state of "eagerness and directed purpose."

This concept of seeking in the brain was developed by Panksepp over the course of several decades spent researching emotional systems in mammals. Essentially, seeking represents our will to act; it explains our most innate drive—that is, the will to wake up every morning and forage for survival.

This instinct is not irreversible. In studies where dopamine neurons are destroyed, starving lab rats presented with food won't even take two steps to eat it, because their wanting system—their motivational circuitry—is no longer functioning. Provided that the rats' pleasure and consummatory pathways are still intact though, these same immobilized rodents *will eat* if food is placed directly in their mouths.

Wanting and liking form a kind of symbiotic loop of motivation and satisfaction. Wanting drives us to pursue the object of our desire. Once we get it, our liking circuits, and the consummatory acts that stimulate them, inhibit our need to seek. This state of satisfaction and calm lasts until these inhibitors wear off, and then we start all over again.

Built to Play

If there's a pattern to the rewards or surprises we encounter, our brain quickly recognizes it. Each time something good happens, neurons in our reward circuitry fire. Over time, though, a special group of prediction neurons start firing at the first sign that a reward is coming. This is the reason Pavlov's dog would salivate at the sound of a bell—his brain knew that a treat was on its way. The more these neurons fire together—the more repeatable the pattern—the more their synapses are strengthened. As they say, neurons that fire together wire together.

This hunt for patterns explains much about the gamer mindset, our Internet addiction, and flow. There is some evidence to suggest that our internal sense of time is also controlled by dopamine, which would explain why flow activities (including playing games) can create the illusion of time flying or standing still.

Rather than thinking of our brain as particularly responsive to play, we might be better off thinking of it as *built for play*. With this in mind, it's not surprising that Panksepp believes the instinct to play actually originates in the human brain stem—the source of our most basic functions. Scientists at Monash University have shown a correlation between brain size and playfulness in mammals: the bigger the brain, the bigger the player. Our massive brain may make us the most playful species of all.

The human brain is an unbelievably complex system that, for all our probing, still retains many mysteries. Even one small area, like the basal ganglia (which plays host to most of the phenomena we discussed here), operates through a tangled web of excitatory, inhibitory, and disinhibitory pathways across half a dozen functional parts. This stuff is anything but simple.

The functional arrangement of billions of neurons in our brains isn't necessarily elegant, but it is breathtakingly effective. And that's simply because our wetware wasn't designed—it evolved in a world that rewards organisms who learn quickly and regularly. To learn, we must venture out to explore and probe the world around us. To motivate that exploration, our brain encourages play.

Play Is a State of Mind

It's tempting to think about play as something we *do*. But play is more elusive than that; it can't be observed as a behavior without some understanding of the participants. For everyone but their owners, two dogs playing vigorously might be indistinguishable from those same dogs fighting. Or put in terms of our own species, when a chef cooks something new, it feels like play. When I cook something new, it feels like work. Both of us are making a meal, but we're not experiencing the same thing. *Play is a state of mind.*

Interestingly, we can come to an activity emotionally ready to play, but an activity also has the ability to prompt a play state in us. For example, try playing dodgeball with your co-workers and remaining even-tempered and unexcited. As students of human behavior, the notion that an activity or stimulus can trigger our natural play response is important, and we'll come back to it later.

Playing with Patterns

Play gives us a chance to hone what we do best (and what we most enjoy): noticing, deciphering, and mastering patterns. It has been suggested by Jeff Hawkins (the founder of Palm), among others, that human intelligence is really nothing more than an extremely sophisticated pattern recognition engine.

In the context of play, that makes an awful lot of sense. Nothing seems to be more satisfying than figuring things out—grokking the rules of any system. In any playful activity, the participant is asking himself, "What must I overcome to achieve my objective?"

Play Is Learning

When we play against obstacles, we make an assumption about what might work, and then test our hypothesis. In this way, all play is an active hunt for a pattern—a hands-on way to train our brains. The uncertainty, resistance, and difficulty we face in different kinds of play create a unique kind of tension. And it's this force that pushes back against our desires and forces us to figure out a way to succeed.

Tension permeates the experience of "probing," a concept that has been discussed by professor James Paul Gee (an expert on games and learning) and Steven Johnson. Probing is simply the act of exploring an environment or phenomenon we don't understand in an orderly way. Gee's account of the probing process, in which he describes players hypothesizing about and testing their virtual environments, sounds incredibly similar to the process we employ in scientific research. Could it be that play is simply an emotionally charged expression of the scientific method? If so, then probing is our most natural learning mechanism.

Gee and other scholars have been making this assertion about game-based learning for years. In talking about the connection between fun, play, and learning he remarks, "When learning stops, fun stops, and playing eventually stops. For humans, real learning is always associated with pleasure, is ultimately a form of play—a principle almost always dismissed by schools." Play isn't a way to make learning fun . . . play *is* learning.

Play Is Misunderstood

At some point in our past, we drew a line between work and play as if they were somehow exclusive concepts. Work is productive, play is frivolous. This may have been an important message when scolding factory workers during the Industrial Revolution, but it's an inaccurate and counterproductive message today amidst the Digital Revolution. Let me contradict a couple centuries of wisdom with a thought of my own: *play is an abundant energy source that powers all human potential.* To tap into it, we need to define it, understand it, and respect it—all difficult activities in a culture that has relegated it to playgrounds and idle hands.

Defining Play

The study of play has a rich recent history, but prior to Johan Huizinga, no one had explored it thoroughly. Huizinga was a Dutch historian and cultural theorist who wrote the seminal book on play in culture entitled *Homo Ludens* (translation: playing man) in 1938. He opens the book with a wake-up call about the nature of play: "Play is older than culture, for culture, however inadequately defined, always presupposes human society, and animals have not waited for man to teach them their playing."

Even though we've all seen animals at play, it's easy to get caught up in the idea that play is a somehow uniquely human experience. Those who haven't observed it carefully may even assume that play is a recent development in our evolution, the result of free time that would be better spent on serious endeavors (mirroring our cultural view on play). Huizinga reminds us though, that play is bigger and older than we think it is.

If play is indeed an ancient and abstract concept, then how might we define it? Huizinga's definition is the most widely cited on the subject. Although many experts have since added their two cents, it's a great starting point for understanding play:

> Summing up the formal characteristic of play, we might call it a free activity standing quite consciously outside "ordinary" life as being "not serious" but at the same time absorbing the player intensely and utterly. It is an activity connected with no material interest, and no profit can be gained by it. It proceeds within its own proper boundaries of time and space according to fixed rules and in an orderly manner. It promotes the formation of social groupings that tend to surround themselves with secrecy and to stress the difference from the common world by disguise or other means.

Huizinga's definition is quite focused on the meaning of play in specific (and human) terms. A more abstract definition from two modern experts on games and play comes from game designers and authors Katie Salen and Eric Zimmerman: "Play is the free space of movement within a more rigid structure." This elegantly frames the concept of play far more broadly, and indeed, works in almost any context. Whether we play with a toy, the guitar, or even a board game, we're embodying this more open-ended definition of the term.

While both of these definitions make sense, it is Huizinga's notion that play occurs outside ordinary life that is crucial to understanding the magic of play. He later describes it as "a stepping out of 'real' life into a temporary sphere of activity with a disposition all its own." It seems Mr. Rogers was right—the Land of Make Believe is where it's at.

Putting the Fun in Play

Not surprisingly, play is fun. And fun is powerful. We all want to have it. If you think back to the best moments of your life, they will almost uniformly be defined by fun. Your first year away from home in the college dorm. Your most recent vacation. Those first few days (and nights) with a new love interest. These experiences are all defined by an intense feeling of enjoyment and elation. Yet fun is surprisingly difficult to describe.

While we all know it when we see it, fun remains ambiguous. In *Homo Ludens*, Huizinga points out that there may not be a truly equivalent word in any other language. So, we're left with limited clarity on the nature of fun, but we do know this: fun is essential.

Or is it? Thinking back to Psychology 101, there's no mention of fun in Abraham Maslow's famous hierarchy of human needs. His landmark paper "A Theory of Human Motivation" outlined five levels of need, progressing in order of sophistication: physiological, safety, love/belonging, esteem, and self-actualization. Accepting Maslow's theory for a second, we should consider why fun might be absent from his list. Perhaps fun isn't a need at all.

Instead, we should consider fun as a means rather than an end. If that's the case, then we should be able to have fun in a wide range of circumstances. We most certainly can. In fact, we need to. Dale Carnegie, in *How to Win Friends and Influence People*, says it all, "People rarely succeed at anything unless they have fun in what they are doing." Of course, it's easier to have fun on a Caribbean vacation than in prison, but fun is not conditional to our circumstance. It can and will occur anywhere.

Fun Is Nature's Reward

Evolutionary psychology tells us that having fun increases our chances of survival. In attempting to explain the joy of being chased in sports like football or tag, Boston College Professor Peter Gray recalls the work of Karl Groos, a naturalist, who wrote *The Play of Animals* in 1898. Groos posited that young mammals who engage in games of chase derive great joy from the activity because repeated games of chase will *prepare them for fleeing from predators.*

Gray suggests that since humans may have evolved in situations where fleeing was necessary, sports like basketball, football, and hockey mimic this same dynamic. In these games a single player transporting a ball or puck attempts to avoid a horde of "enemies" in order to score. So, according to Groos, *fun is nature's reward for practicing survival skills.* That makes having fun seem a lot less trivial.

Fun Can Be Hard

As play becomes harder and more intense (especially in the case of modern video games), the fun we experience feels different. In 1989 a small boy playing with LEGOs during a research session at the MIT Media Lab coined the term "hard fun" to describe the way he felt in constructing a complicated structure. Seymour Papert and others at the lab later popularized the term.

Hard fun suggests the distinction between fun as pleasure (a roller coaster ride), and fun as enjoyment (building a beautiful sand castle), in which the latter is clearly the hard fun. Hard fun has the potential to be infinitely more rewarding, and is the by-product of a well-designed game.

What Now?

A lot of what makes us human is hardwired. Our brains, like neurological Venus flytraps, will spring into action if we stimulate them in the right way. I find myself constantly wondering: what would it take to trigger the people around me, and get them to play along? If we can motivate millions *inside* games, could we get them to do other, more positive things in the "real world"? Must all of our best motivational levers be trapped in *video* games?

Of course not. Games are simply the one place where a basic understanding of psychological and sociological forces is being put to practical use in designing experiences.

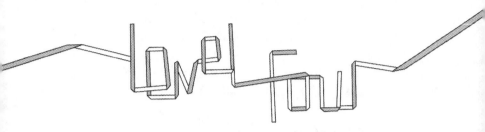

Level Four

We are in love with the new. Whether it's an all new episode of our favorite TV show, a new car, or a new friend, we go out of our way for novelty. That's why marketers like Gillette started introducing variations of classic products in the first place. We didn't actually need a razor with five blades, we just needed a *new razor* to covet.

Our brain's seeking circuits are particularly sensitive to novelty (anything surprising or unexpected). Even the *anticipation* of something new stirs us. When something novel happens, like a promotion we weren't expecting, or a satisfying twist in our favorite television show, it triggers a dopamine boost (and some opioids as well) that effectively tells our brain, "That was amazing. Now why did it happen and how can we make it happen again?"

In terms of novelty, games are incredibly rich territory. Good games give you countless features to unlock or discover, including new weapons, new levels, and new characters. Beyond that, games unfold a narrative in which you are the protagonist— where your willingness to explore leads to more and more adventure. As Steven Johnson says in *Everything Bad Is Good for You,* "Most of the time, when you're hooked on a game, what draws you in is an elemental form of desire: the desire to *see the next thing.*" It's the same feeling we experience when watching a great movie or TV series, but with one important twist: in games, you move things along. You set the pace.

The ultimate surprise in gaming comes from achieving an "epic win." What's that? Jane McGonigal describes it beautifully: "An epic win is an outcome that is so extraordinarily positive you had no idea it was even possible until you achieved it." Understandably, when you accomplish the unthinkable in this way, your brain chemistry goes nuts. And the most feasible and likely place to do something that spectacular is, of course, in a game.

Getting to Know Games

So what *is* a game? We've made it this far, but a clear definition of our subject matter still eludes us. Games are everywhere, but their characteristics aren't so apparent. To better understand, let's review a few common threads, followed by a popular definition of the term.

A Game Demands Participation

Many forms of entertainment require less of us than games do. When you read a book or watch a movie you have to make sense of the story, but not *interact* with it. You may have to choose how to imagine a character or scene, or form an opinion about how the story makes you feel, but you don't have to explicitly choose what happens next.

Games on the other hand, require players to actively participate in determining the course of events. The difference is well illustrated in the juxtaposition between fans and players at a football game; the fans watch the events unfold, but nothing changes if they stop to get a hot dog. The players have to create the game one play at a time, and if they stop, so does the game.

A Game Can Be Played Again

One thing that separates games from other forms of entertainment is that they're renewable. You can play ten thousand games of chess in a lifetime and each one will be slightly different. On top of that, every successive game will likely be more interesting than the last, due to ever-increasing skills and a heightened perception of the experience.

Compare that to your favorite television show or movie. How many times can you watch one of those before it becomes boring? Two or three times easily, but certainly not a thousand. And of course, a movie is always exactly the same, every time you watch it.

A Game Is Understood Through Play

Telling a friend about a game isn't likely to thrill them, because a description of a game is often boring and in many cases incomprehensible. This is why my mother rolls her eyes when my brother describes a round of golf in painstaking detail. *You had to be there.* Hearing about making a game-winning shot in basketball is nothing compared to the feeling of that first swish. Ultimately, the only way to truly understand a game—any game—is to play it for yourself.

Easy to Play, Hard To Define

In *Rules of Play*, Katie Salen and Eric Zimmerman thoroughly explore the nature of games, and outline the subtleties and challenges of defining them. As part of their process, they round up and analyze definitions from a wide range of game scholars, illustrating the variation among them. Even between these experts, there exists division about the importance of basic concepts such as rules, conflict, goals, make-believe, and voluntary participation. In evaluating these differences, Salen and Zimmerman show an evolution of thought within the industry and deliver a blended definition made sharper by the group's many attempts:

> A game is a system in which players engage in an artificial conflict, defined by rules, that results in a quantifiable outcome.

35

This definition works well, and covers everything from video games to board games and sports. As we consider how games might help us find volition and faculty in our daily lives, one piece of the definition stands out above the rest and is reminiscent of Huizinga's definition of play: the notion of an artificial conflict. It's common knowledge that games aren't real—that they require imagination on our part. Understanding that dynamic is crucial to bridging the gap between the virtual and the real.

The Magic Circle

The separation of games from reality is so fundamental that game designers have a term for it: the magic circle. To understand it, let's talk about Monopoly money.

I hate to break it to you, but Monopoly money isn't real. Yet even knowing this, it still feels great when someone hands you one of those orange $500 bills during the game. In fact, just watching how other people handle and sort their money in the game signals its significance to them. For some reason, when we're playing Monopoly, the play money matters. Why?

As it turns out, when we play games we enter a sort of "alternate universe" where we accept the rules and constraints of a new imaginary world. Think about it. In Monopoly, you accept everything from the rules about paying rent, to collecting $200 when you pass go, to going straight to jail if a "chance card" tells you to.

It's no different in other games. In *World of Warcraft*, you have to accept that you are a mythical being, and that quests and raids might be an important part of your virtual day. The point is, when you sit down to play, you're using your imagination to escape reality and accept something that your rational mind would never allow. Poet Samuel Taylor Coleridge coined the term "willing suspension of disbelief" to describe this phenomenon in literature, but it applies equally well in any medium.

This psychological space—where games are played—is what game scholars mean when they refer to the magic circle. It was

Huizinga who made first mention of this term in *Homo Ludens*. That notion was built upon by several generations of game designers and academics who have since expanded and enriched the concept.

According to them, the magic circle is a state of mind that you allow yourself to enter when you begin a game. In many cases, the acceptance of the magic circle is aided by real world cues, such as the specified markings of a court in the game of basketball or a checkered board in chess. When you step into that space, you're in the game's world. This idea makes the transition from reality to the game world a clear one. It's the reason that people are so interested in understanding the rules of a new game—they're trying to establish the boundaries of the magic circle.

What's most important to understand about this concept is that it's a choice. You choose to enter the magic circle and work within it. While there, you know deep down that it's artificial, but you repress that knowledge and revel in the adventure. Imagination is a powerful thing.

One of our greatest strengths (and weaknesses) is that we can convince ourselves of anything . . . even things that are statistically impossible.

All the Children Are Above Average

At least, that's the way the story goes. Garrison Keillor has famously concluded every tale of his fictional town with the same line for decades, ". . . and that's the news from Lake Wobegon, where all the women are strong, all the men are good looking, and all the children are above average." His humorous poke at our tendency to make positive generalizations belies a powerful insight about human nature.

In the wild, being above average can mean the difference between eating and not eating, mating and not mating—even life and death. So it makes sense that we covet this status. In fact, we spend a significant amount of time evaluating our place in the pecking order for any number of traits and skills. "Am I the prettiest one in the room? The smartest? The wealthiest?" We make snap judgments about our status all the time, and we base our social interactions around those assessments. "Who is going to get the promotion? Well, let's see, I'm a far better performer than Tim, but Katie gives me a run for my money."

Our Distorted View

This intense desire to be better than the rest has some interesting side effects. The concept of illusory superiority (also known as the Lake Wobegon effect) demonstrates that we tend to think we're better than we actually are. For example, in 2000, a whopping 87 percent of students in Stanford University's MBA program rated their academic performance above the median. In an earlier study, 68 percent of University of Nebraska faculty rated themselves in the top 25 percent for teaching ability.

And these effects aren't limited to academia. Studies have shown that we tend to rate our own relationships, our popularity, and our health better than average. A survey done in the United States and Sweden showed that 93 percent of Americans and 69 percent of Swedes ranked themselves in the top 50 percent for driving skills. Of course, rationally we know this simply can't be; *everyone* can't be above average at the same time. Yet individually, we still believe we belong in the upper half.

Examining this effect more closely, researchers Justin Kruger and David Dunning devised a series of experiments that took into account the level of skill of each participant in how they ranked themselves. They found that unskilled and ignorant participants tended to overestimate their own skills, whereas trained participants more accurately rated or even underestimated their abilities. Ironically, those who didn't know much thought they knew everything, and those who knew plenty thought they had a lot to learn. Also intriguing were findings that different cultures manifest this bias in different ways. Japanese students, for example, believed that they were better than other Japanese students *in general,* but not better than their own classmates, an interesting twist reflecting the nuance of culture.

Optimism Is a Good Thing

Regardless of cultural differences, why might we maintain a distorted view of our place in the world? As is often the case with any persistent trait, it's probably necessary for survival. Waking up every day and taking on the world requires an incredible amount of optimism. If we truly didn't believe that we were going to make a better life, we'd quickly lose hope and just wait for the end to come. Luckily, illusory superiority and other "helpful" delusions give us the outlook we need to face it all.

Research examining expectations for the future showed that people tend to believe that a greater number of good things (job promotions, gifted children, a long life, etc.) await them versus the average person. That's pretty good motivation to keep going. Another potential explanation comes once again from the perspective of evolutionary psychology. In life, we start out ignorant and without skills. A boost of confidence ensures that we take action and continue to learn and achieve. As our skills mature, as in the Kruger and Dunning study, slightly *under*estimating our abilities can lead to even more sustained effort in pursuit of mastery.

One thing is certain: anything worth doing is hard to master, and it's not always clear what steps we must take to improve. There isn't a guidebook for each and every skill, and even if there was, reading and *doing* are two very different things. Beyond the challenges of basic self-improvement, becoming better than average is harder still. In many cases, it's not even clear where we stand. Can you accurately place how you'd rank in a footrace with all your co-workers? Unlikely. And yet while a footrace is probably irrelevant, this kind of ambiguity permeates our lives, and can be quite frustrating.

Just Like You, Only Better

If feeling superior in some way is part of our subjective well-being, then it's not surprising that many of us retreat to the world of video games to feel good about ourselves. These games offer us much in our quest to avoid the obscurity of averageness. Rather than replicate the real world where our deficiencies are often laid bare, they let us play as a different and better version of ourselves. Almost every popular video game of the last ten years has given us the chance to be someone extraordinary. We might have magical powers, unbelievable strength, battle armor, or the ability to pilot a heavily armed fighter plane. Plugging in gives us access to a kind of instant status, even if it is only temporary and imaginary.

But far more important than the avatar we control is the process of self-improvement offered in games of every genre, from a role-playing action game like *Mass Effect* to an exercise game like *Wii Fit*. From the moment we begin, these games are designed to challenge us with tasks that will help us acquire skills, demonstrate mastery, and move on to the next level. This concept of achieving a certain status and moving up in the game world is known as "leveling up" and is such a powerful idea that it permeates gamer culture.

Why is leveling up so straightforward in games? Because these systems are designed with our love of progress in mind. Games give us information about our developing skills in the form of real-time feedback, points, leaderboards, and dozens of other clever mechanisms. Rather than letting our illusory superiority run rampant, they force us to face facts, press on, and earn our way into the standings by completing tasks that match and then challenge our level of skill. It's no wonder we have a culture of gamers who are obsessed with leveling up in every aspect of their lives. We all want to believe we're above average, and if we can somehow raise our profile, that belief is justified.

Why Do We Love Games?

I think we all wish life were a little bit more like a game. Perhaps we yearn for that crowd of fans that would support us as if we were players on the field. Or maybe we like the idea of extra lives. Or a soundtrack to our every move. The ability to risk it all and know that nothing can hurt us. But back here in reality, most of that isn't so. What are the key characteristics of games that turn us on?

Games Can Happen Anywhere

Games allow us to have hard fun and create engaging experiences whenever and wherever we want. This year I had the pleasure of taking an audio tour of Alcatraz Island in San Francisco. At one point during the tour, a former inmate explained that to pass the time in solitary confinement, he'd take a coin or button and throw it aimlessly into the pitch darkness of his cell. Then he'd go about the laborious task of trying to find it. Once found, he'd simply do it all over again. This survival mechanism was desperate, but an effective attempt to create a game in difficult circumstances.

Games Give Us Purpose

In a world where priorities are hard to determine and even harder to keep straight, games give us a clear sense of purpose. While more traditional games promote winning as a common goal, interactive games tend to promote more complex and satisfying ambitions that tap into our desire to be heroes.

For most of us, aligning our day jobs with our life's purpose is downright difficult. In games, your purpose is aligned with your tasks by design. In your quest to save the princess, many tasks await you, but ultimately, they're going to add up to saving the lady you love. It's hard to believe you're serving a higher purpose when you're filing an expense report.

GAME FRAME

We Solve Problems in Games

Do you know what the bane of a third-grade math student's existence is? A word problem. But somehow, these same students are able to comprehend infinitely more complex concepts in games. In his book *Good Video Games and Good Learning*, James Paul Gee discusses the complexity of the role-playing card game *Yu-Gi-Oh*. The game contains over ten thousand individual cards, each one with a functional role based on a complex specialist language. Gee refers to these communications as a "lucidly functional language"—meaning that the words derive their meaning from the actions they imply. He gives a brief example of the complexity with one sentence from the Yu-Gi-Oh website referring to a specific card, the 8-Claws Scorpion: "Even if '8-Claws Scorpion' is equipped with an Equip Spell Card, its ATK is 2400 when it attacks a face-down Defense Position Monster."

You got that? Most seven-year-olds who play the game could walk you through that and a hundred other cards before breakfast. Yet they struggle with fractions. The game *should* be making them better math students, but their *Yu-Gi-Oh* skills are useless in math class.

Regardless, games inspire critical thinking: many MMOs and console games ask players to participate in long-term nested problem solving. That includes scenarios in which players have an "ultimate" goal that is unachievable without first completing several smaller tasks. These sub-missions must be discovered through the course of playing the game. For example, if you want to save the princess, first you must cross the river. To do that, you need to build a boat. To do that, you need lumber. To get that, you need an axe, and so on. In many of today's popular titles this chain of tasks and puzzles can be hundreds of items long. Whether it be twenty, forty, or even one hundred hours of play later, most committed gamers emerge victorious.

It's safe to say that very few real world problems get this kind of attention. In *Everything Bad is Good For You*, Steven Johnson goes so far as to propose that nested problems like these are actually making us smarter—raising the average IQ—a phenomenon known as the Flynn effect. According to Johnson, the cognitive complexity presented by popular television shows, movies, and video games in the last decade far outweighs the content of the previous generation. Considering all forms of media as puzzles to be solved, our brains have had to rise to the challenge of deeper and more nested storylines.

Games Give Us Control

In addition to purpose, games offer us control. A key part of our early development is rooted in this idea: that we each have the ability to interact with the world around us and shape it in some small way. Children quickly learn that when they push a toy car, it rolls away. This kind of agency is fascinating to them as they make sense of the world around them. Yet, somewhere along the way to adulthood, our desire for control expands beyond our grasp, and many people feel powerless in the world.

In video games, though, we are given the goals we need to achieve and all the control that we need to pursue them. We can easily figure out how the world of the game "works." Everything we're capable of has been planned for in some way, and the system gives us feedback on our efforts. This is why so much learning is happening in games; learning isn't tedious if it's happening in pursuit of a goal.

This concept of control goes hand-in-hand with the notion of an ideal world, one that Steven Poole describes in *Trigger Happy* as "the temporary perfection, unattainable in the physical world, of absolute order." We love games because they show us a predictable meritocracy, an orderly world in which we have all the faculty we need to pursue our goals.

Games Show Us Progress

In a recent study published in the *Harvard Business Review*, Teresa Amabile and Steven Kramer set out to discover what really motivates workers. As you'd expect, most of the managers they surveyed believed that recognition or incentives were the best motivators. They were wrong. As it turns out, the best motivator and mood elevator of all was . . . progress. When people felt as though they were making strides at work, or getting support from higher-ups to remove obstacles, they were happier and more driven to succeed.

Of course, game designers have known this for a long time. The feedback that games give, in terms of levels and achievements, is progress, plain and simple. In terms of challenging work, we derive our satisfaction not from the moment, but from pausing to look back and see how far we've come. Doing the same job every day might pass for progress in the real world, but as a game, that would be unbearable.

We Take Risks In Games

When's the last time you tried to jump from one rooftop to another? Unless you're a practitioner of parkour, I hope the answer is never. What about quitting your job to start that company you're always talking about? Chances are less than 1 percent that you'll do that this year. Why? Because humans are risk averse, and rightfully so. Miss that roof-to-roof jump, and you're in the hospital. Start a company that makes widgets nobody needs, and your kids will have no money for college. Real choices have real consequences, and the world doesn't have a "do over" button. While this makes sense, it's also tragic. Because risk is an important part of progress. We learn from trial and error. But if we're too afraid to try, we never get the chance to learn.

I was recently reminded how opposed to trial and error our culture can be. This year, in order to apply for a specific high school class, my stepbrother was required to take an entrance exam. If he took the test and succeeded, he'd be able to take the class and learn the material. If he failed, he'd be denied entrance before the class even started. Needless to say, he wasn't thrilled with this arrangement.

Can you imagine if a game you bought at the store worked this way? You plunk down fifty bucks for it and take it home. You boot it up on your Xbox. You're just beginning to walk around and explore this new world when BAM, you're shot. Game over. Your Xbox spits the game out, and it's unplayable thereafter. How long do you think *this* game developer would be in business?

Games don't have this problem. They're built to reset, reload, and start over. They even pioneered the concept of extra lives. Games want us to take risks. They want us to learn. And we do. We accomplish more in games because we play with abandon. And with that freedom comes the deep joy of learning and progress.

Games Let Us Face Our Fears

Not only do games let us take risks, but they can make those risks feel real. In *Exodus to the Virtual World*, Edward Castronova shares research that suggests our brain doesn't differentiate between media images and real images (at first blush). What this means is that when you see an explosion during a video game, your brain doesn't *automatically* assume it's not real. That reality check happens after you initially process the image. Your brain has no innate way of knowing what's real and what isn't—not that long ago, everything we saw *was* real.

This process of evaluation makes it possible for our higher-level brain to "choose" to back off when we watch a movie or play a game. We willingly enter into the illusion of a game and feel the fear of taking risks as if they were real. However, while real fear is arousing, it can also be debilitating. In games and other entertainment, we experience a kind of mediated fear.

Indiana University professor Andrew Weaver describes the power of fear-inducing media in similar terms: "Experiencing mediated fear gives us the opportunity to experience fear in a controlled way. Where we have the potential, at least, to master our fears, to control threats, in a way that we can't in real life." So then, if we can master our fears in games, can we subvert our instincts as well?

Consider how Secret Service agents prepare for duty. To do their job correctly, an agent assigned to the president must be willing to take a bullet for the commander in chief. But when push comes to shove, it's hard to undo millions of years of instinct telling us to avoid bodily harm. So how do they do it? They simulate it—over and over again.

So much of preparing for any potentially violent job is in the rehearsal. Through the use of imaginative play, the agents' brains are slowly rewired to react differently to a situation that would have you or me hitting the deck. Through repetition, games teach us to take mediated risks and, sometimes, real ones.

Games Give Us the Glory

We all want to matter. But in a world with over 6 billion people, it's easy to question whether we do. Sitting through a staff meeting or an algebra class, it's normal to wonder if this is all meaningless. Games are a powerful escape from that uncertainty.

In a game, you are the chosen one, selected to lead your troops across the ocean, or to stop the spread of the undead zombies who have taken over your town. Because of this, games give us a sense of incredible meaning and importance in an alternate reality. Being a hero in real life takes training, time, and even a little luck. Being a hero in video games requires only that you power up your Xbox.

Along the lines of heroism is the idea of glory. Related to our competitive drive, the glory of winning is a powerful motivator. Glory is not about winning privately, though. It's about winning in the presence of a social group that recognizes our victory. Glory, like honor, is bestowed by those around us, and carried on by those who come after us. In this way, games—particularly competitive games—offer us a modern chance to grab some glory. Sometimes this social recognition is the most valuable thing we can obtain. The joy of soundly trouncing a member of your peer group in almost any game is hard to match.

LEVEL FOUR

Games Shift Time

We've all heard the saying, "Time flies when you're having fun." But we know that the contrary is true, as well. The experience of certain activities leaves us to wonder after an evening flies by, where did the time go? At the same time, many people report that during certain activities time stands still, and a five-minute performance can feel like an eternity (in a good way). For many players, games transform time into an illusion.

In a recent study by Simon Tobin and Simon Grondin at the Université Laval, adolescents were asked to estimate the amount of time that had passed during an eight-minute Tetris game as well as an eight-minute reading exercise. As you'd expect, the game experience was consistently estimated to be shorter than the reading experience. As we've seen, this is one of the key indicators of flow—the feeling that time has been transformed.

But the passage of time can also have an effect on how we perceive activities, including games. A recent series of studies by Aaron Sackett of the University of St. Thomas asked participants to perform a task that took them roughly ten minutes to complete. Once done, the participants were told one of two things: either that only five minutes had passed, or that twenty minutes had gone by. They found that when people believed time had gone by quickly (such as the people who did ten minutes of work and were told it was twenty), they rated those experiences as being more enjoyable. Those who believed time had dragged on rated the same activity as less enjoyable. These findings also applied to how much participants enjoyed songs, and even how irritating they found loud noises to be.

This research confirms an interesting twist on a familiar saying. Time flies when you're having fun. And you *think* you're having fun when time flies.

GAME FRAME

Games Bring Us Together

We've discussed several reasons why we love games, but perhaps the most important reason of all is that they bring us together. Games, although they can be played individually, become especially powerful when they're social activities.

Throughout history they have connected us, united us, and given us common language and purpose. After a good game, we'll sit and talk over drinks to discuss the events of the day. We'll lament our mistakes and savor our victories. We'll laugh together. Undoubtedly, games are the domain of friends.

What Happens in Games Doesn't Stay There

All these benefits underscore the fact that what's happening in the game world is coming back with us to the real world. A recent study by Daphne Bavelier, who previously showed that games increase our ability to detect objects in a cluttered space, is now suggesting that games can actually improve contrast sensitivity in the eye, something previously only possible with the use of prescription glasses or surgery. And this improvement was not small. We're talking about a 58 percent increase compared to people who did not play the games in the study, namely *Call of Duty* and *Unreal Tournament*.

And of course, along with these physiological changes come cognitive ones as well. The whole notion of persuasive games suggests that games have the power to shape our attitudes, beliefs, and even our thoughts. In one inventive example, research subjects were asked to play a cycling game to test a new sports drink delivery mechanism. When a teammate passed them in the game, they received a shot of juice from a straw in their mouths. When an enemy player passed them in the game, they got a shot of salty tea. Both teammates and enemies wore jerseys decorated with specific insignia. Days later in a waiting area, these same participants *subconsciously* avoided sitting in a chair that bore the insignia of the enemy team's jersey. It was as if they had been programmed to avoid it.

For business managers who question the role of games in shaping good employees, this quote from *The Kids Are Alright*, by John C. Beck and Mitchell Wade, is particularly intriguing: "Odds are that the more you played games as a youngster, the more you care about the company you work for." While younger generations are known for job-hopping, these authors are suggesting that gamers are mimicking the challenge-seeking behavior that they learned from games. But they do have the potential to form more meaningful organizational attachments given the right conditions. If their company is on an engaging and meaningful mission, and their role in that quest is clear, they'll be loyal to a fault.

Games Represent What Could Be

Given all that we've seen about the nature of games, we can no longer accept that they are simply a mindless escape from reality. Rather, they represent a mind*ful* escape from so many poorly structured experiences. Games offer us a glimpse of a *better* world, one that in many cases mirrors our own. Whether it be sports, board games, or video games, games represent the world as we would like it to be: challenging, forgiving, dynamic—a world where every one of us is a hero in our own story.

Games are getting serious. Prompted by the realization that games are powerful learning engines, academic institutions and corporations have begun to experiment with new concepts of gaming, most notably the area of "serious games," which are designed for a purpose beyond entertainment. Serious games are already used in many fields, including education, marketing, health care, city planning, engineering, defense, and politics.

Looking back on my days playing *Oregon Trail*, I can see that it was an educational progenitor of many serious games to come. Other early roots can be found in the military, where war games have been played for centuries, educating soldiers and testing new strategies. Today, serious games are everywhere, but sometimes hard to spot. They tend to be created for a few practical purposes: solving problems, creating predictions, and training/education. New applications are cropping up every day.

In the field of medical research, determining how complex proteins fold and structure themselves is extremely important, as it may lead to breakthroughs in treating diseases like HIV, malaria, and cancer. But determining how to fold complex proteins is a challenging process, even for computers. For some reason, though, human intuition in this area is actually quite good. That's why a team of academics and researchers working in connection with the University of Washington created a serious game called *Foldit*. In the game, users are presented with partially folded protein structures and asked to continue folding them according to specific rules, in a kind of three-dimensional puzzle game.

The process is challenging and fun, but also meaningful. As tens of thousands of players complete their puzzles, the solutions most likely to represent possible real-world breakthroughs are sent back to headquarters to be evaluated for merit. Meanwhile, *Foldit*'s players are getting better and better. In a recent head-to-head challenge, they beat a rival computer system called Rosetta five out of ten times, and ended with a draw on another three.

Prediction markets are another popular form of serious game. In these environments, players are given a certain amount of virtual currency or votes and asked to invest them in the outcomes they see as most likely to occur. Often, the future can be more accurately predicted by a crowd versus a lone prognosticator. For example, both Microsoft and Google have been known to use prediction markets to identify accurate release dates for their software products.

Finally, in *Persuasive Games*, Ian Bogost makes reference to the training software used at Cold Stone Creamery, a chain of ice cream stores. At Cold Stone, they use a game to help new employees learn about portion control, waste, and overall profitability. Rather than seeing a slightly large scoop as a small one-time issue, the game shows the implications of that scoop if it were replicated across the entire enterprise. Suddenly a ten cent mistake becomes a ten-thousand-dollar one. The game, called *Stone City* (in reference to the popular simulation *Sim City*), allows this lesson to occur in a zero-cost high-engagement environment, rather than in the store with customers waiting. Only after that procedural learning has taken place virtually is it reinforced in reality, with real scoops.

At this moment serious games are being developed for almost every conceivable industry and application. These games are effective, and in many cases reduce risk and cost in areas where we currently have a lot of both. It's an important and expanding genre in the world of gaming, and if you haven't experienced it firsthand in your education or career just yet, you probably will soon.

The Age of Data

The same organizations that are putting serious games to use are also part of a growing trend of data collection and analysis. Right now, as you go about your daily life, much of your behavior is being tracked, recorded, and analyzed. Surprised? You shouldn't be.

We are living in the age of data. It's now possible to measure almost anything, and that information has become indispensable. Your credit card company has a record of every dollar you've spent, including where and when you spent it. Your Internet service provider knows what websites you're visiting and what you're doing on them. Google knows what you're searching for, and if you found it. Your mobile carrier (and several of your apps) know where you are nearly every moment of the day. Facebook knows how many friends you have, and how often you're communicating with them. Pandora knows what music you like. And Netflix knows what movies you've watched, and how much you'll like movies you *haven't even seen yet.*

But what good is all this knowledge?

If you're highly skilled at crunching numbers, then knowledge is power. Because raw data, when analyzed properly, can lead to important insights, opportunities, and lasting competitive advantage. Having always known this intuitively, we're now seeing this idea take hold. Large brands are hiring more and more graduates with expertise in data modeling and analytics, in the hopes that they can predict the future of the stock market, weather, TV ratings, and product popularity. They're using behavioral targeting in an attempt to reach consumers with marketing messages at precisely the right place and time. IBM recently overhauled its whole communications strategy to focus on the simple but powerful idea of a "smarter planet," offering their vision of a data-rich future for cities, health care, food, energy, and more than a dozen other categories. The IBM website shares the concept in three phases: "instrument the world's systems, interconnect them, make them intelligent." While they might be the first to put it so clearly, they're not alone. The global data craze is truly just beginning.

In his book *Super Crunchers*, Ian Ayres shares the story of Orley Ashenfelter, an economist at Princeton who found a way to predict the quality of a Bordeaux wines based on the weather. Orley determined that in years with high temperatures and low rainfall, Bordeaux wines tend to be more concentrated and delicious. So, he devised a formula that accounted for these variables and their relative impact on price. The best part? Orley had the data he needed as soon as the season was over, compared to regular aficionados who have to wait months or years for a taste in order to evaluate quality. Although he encountered some friction with the broader community of wine aficionados for describing their art form with simple math, the wine investors who subscribed to Orley's advice consistently outperformed the market.

Having access to this level of sophisticated data and information might be novel to most businesses, but it's old hat to gamers. After all, video games have always given us quick and accurate feedback on our performance. When we play games, we always know where we stand. The Internet, with its ratings, comments, and real-time analytics, is much the same. So it's not surprising that many among us, and gamers especially, have become a bit addicted to data.

Know Thyself

Once limited to the geeky few, the idea of tracking our own data for personal insight is becoming popular, even mainstream. Individuals are becoming more interested in their personal data stream in an attempt to both protect it and use it for their own purposes. In response to this, Gary Wolf and Kevin Kelly started a site called The Quantified Self, which celebrates the people and technologies that are making "self-knowledge through numbers" a reality. According to Wolf, there are four reasons why personal data's time has come:

> Electronic sensors are smaller, better, and cheaper than ever before.
> Mobile phones are more powerful, and more prevalent.
> Social media have made oversharing a habit for millions.
> Cloud computing is putting all this data where everyone can get at it.

Not surprisingly, the number of consumer technologies made expressly for tracking data is exploding. Curious people everywhere have only to spend a few dollars and a few minutes to begin reaping the benefits of personalized data.

What kinds of products and services are out there? Well, there are the usual suspects: speedometers, pedometers, sports watches, heart rate monitors, calorie counters, accelerometers, and finance trackers. And there are more exotic options as well: ovulation trackers, glucose monitors, devices that measure brain waves for concentration and focus, sleep trackers that tell you how much (and what kind of) sleep you're getting, and even a recent patent filing by Sony for a system that will detect the emotional state of people playing games and watching video content. For those adverse to more hardware, dozens of apps that replicate many of these products are available in the iTunes app store right now. Of course, there are also countless websites that track eating and drinking habits, mood, productivity, and other variables (mostly based on self-report). Many of these sites integrate social features as well, allowing users to support and encourage each other.

As measuring the quantifiable aspects of our lives becomes standard, inventive minds will begin to tackle the less quantifiable parts. In this era of rapid research and development, it's hard to conceive of something we couldn't find a way to track. Even something as mysterious as love has a measurable signature in the brain. This notion of detecting the unmeasurable has powerful implications; exposure to data and information we've never seen before (like a real-time measure of employee loyalty) could influence behavior overnight.

One current example demonstrates that our level of interest in a conversation is hiding in our voice. Two researchers at the MIT Media Lab, Anmol Madan and Alex Pentland, created a real-time speech feature analysis application that can tell whether someone is paying attention during a phone call based on intonation and speech patterns. The software, jokingly dubbed the *Jerk-o-Meter*, listens to a conversation and provides feedback ranging from, "Stop being a jerk!" to "Wow, you're a smooth talker." Their software can even predict outcomes, such as whether one of the talkers will agree to go on a date with the other, with 75–85 percent accuracy. This technology, while still nascent, hints at a future where we won't have to guess how our dates are going— we'll just place our phone on the table and see how we're scoring.

Who Really Cares?

Regardless of what is being measured, *someone* can find a way to profit from every single data point. Something as basic as how many steps you're taking each day could be valuable to your health insurance company, life insurance company, employer, footwear brand, sock brand, city planner, and podiatrist. And that's just one piece of information! Multiply that by the thousands of activities you undertake every day, and you can begin to see just how valuable your information might be.

Sensors Everywhere

If our personal data is so valuable to others—and the ability to influence our behavior is even more so—what happens next? Some futurists believe that in the not-too-distant future, we're likely to see inexpensive digital sensors become components of even the most common and disposable household items. Your watch will know when you meet someone new and shake his hand. Your soda can will know when it's being sipped. Your lights will know when you've arrived home. Your television will know if you think NBC's new sitcom is funny. And the trash can on the corner will know when it's full, and that 15 percent of its contents should have been recycled.

In this future, everything you do will be monitored. You'll receive feedback from the system on how you're doing. And when behaviors beget feedback loops—you guessed it—people start to play.

The Gamepocalypse

In *Exodus to the Virtual World*, Edward Castronova describes a future in which the influence of games and virtual experiences has fundamentally changed the way businesses operate and engage employees:

> Suppose we have a delivery company that is organized like a contemporary massively multiplayer game. Here's how it would work . . . [a] new worker would be invited to choose a class to occupy, such as Truck Driver, Sorter, Label-Reader, Pilot, Mechanic, Customer Service Representative, Accountant, etc. Each of these classes would be given a list of activities to complete and rewards for doing them. Drivers might get a list that says "Deliver a small package (five pounds or less) on time, one hundred points. Deliver a large package (more than five pounds) on time, two hundred points. For every ten successful on-time deliveries in a row, receive fifty extra points." Those points would accumulate frequently too, providing the worker with the same kind of steady stream of positive reinforcement that games give. Scan a package, get a point. Answer a complaint email, get three points. Find a lost item, get one hundred points. Points would be used for buying resources within the company, and leftovers would be turned into wages. These reward schedules would be balanced in the sense that a normally talented person who put some energy into the position would net enough points to make a good living.

GAME FRAME

For many people in their twenties and thirties, this notion of a job mixed with a game is incredibly attractive. It implies a linear relationship between effort and reward, and creates structure out of what can be a confusing and illogical workplace. Of course, the challenge with an idea like this lies in designing the game such that it consistently produces positive results for the employees *and* the company. As is often the case with ideas whose time has come, Castronova isn't the only one imagining a world dominated by gaming.

In early 2010, Professor Jesse Schell gave an incendiary speech at the D.I.C.E. Summit outlining a similar vision of the future that he has since referred to as the *Gamepocalypse*. Schell's prophecy extends far beyond the workplace, and serves the agendas of countless brands and organizations. It's no longer simply about the needs and desires of the employer. Instead, it's an ever-present point-based system that attempts to serve the needs and desires of *every* organization, from the corporation to the government to the family unit. In essence, it's a truly *ubiquitous* game, predicated upon the spread of sensors into our most basic household items. He described the future accordingly in his speech:

> You'll get up in the morning to brush your teeth and the toothbrush can sense that you're brushing your teeth. So hey, good job for you, 10 points for brushing your teeth. And it can measure how long, and you're supposed to brush your teeth for 3 minutes. You did! Good job! You brushed your teeth for 3 minutes. So you get a bonus for that. And hey, you brushed your teeth every day this week, another bonus! And who cares? The toothpaste company. The toothbrush company. The more you brush, the more toothpaste you use. They have a vested financial interest.

So here we have this simple idea that even the most banal behavior in your day, brushing your teeth, has value to a corporation. If they can influence your behavior in the "game" then it's supposedly a mutually beneficial arrangement. You have good dental hygiene and some points to show for it. They have higher sales, because you run out of toothpaste faster. Leaving ethics aside for a second, it sounds like a fairly quid pro quo arrangement. But there are so many other situations to consider. Schell expands the story:

> Then you go and get on the bus. The bus? Why am I taking the bus? You're taking the bus because the government has started giving out all kinds of bonus points to people who use public transportation, and you can use these points for tax incentives. . . . And you get to work on time. Good job! Excellent! . . . And then you've got a meeting at another building that's a half a mile away. And you could take the shuttle over, but you thought, "I'm going to walk" because the health insurance plan that you're on gives you bonus points if you walk, like, more than a mile each day, and we can sense that easily, you know, through your digital shoes.

At this point in the story, many people feel that this vision of the future is a bit dystopian—that all these influenced choices reduce us to nothing more than corporate and political shills. Indeed, it's hard to imagine a world in which every decision you make is an economic one—where the choice with the most points is always the victor.

Is the existence of a Gamepocalypse even technologically possible? If the advancements of the last ten years are any indication, anything is conceivable. In fact, before Schell took the stage at D.I.C.E., Oral B had already released the SmartSeries 5000 electric toothbrush. The system includes a separate digital display that tracks brushing in thirty second intervals and guides users through the four quadrants of the mouth.

The connection of smart sensors in our toothbrushes and footwear to some kind of behavioral currency may seem improbable and even intrusive today, but a far more intimate application of sensor technology is already on the horizon.

Brains and Machines

A recent innovation suggests an elegant interface between humans and games that goes beyond the visions of Castronova and Schell. That innovation is the emerging field of brain-computer interfaces (BCI).

The BCI industry is made up of a field of researchers and companies aiming to, at least in part, turn your brain into the ultimate remote control. The idea of a true brain-computer interface came about in the 1970s, and since then many invasive methods (putting hardware in direct contact with the brain) have been used to connect brain to machine.

But it wasn't until a few years ago that the prospect of noninvasive mind control started to become really feasible. Using EEG technology in the form of electromagnetic sensors, researchers have developed headsets that can detect alpha, beta, gamma, and delta waves in the brain and use these signals to wirelessly trigger nearby digital devices. This means that soon, at least in theory, our games will have the potential to read our minds.

I Can Move Things with My Mind

One early commercial example of this technology is the Star Wars Force Trainer. It's a relatively affordable toy that allows users to control the levitation of a ping-pong ball by concentrating on how high they want it to hover.

I braved the crowds at Toys"R"Us during the holidays to buy a Force Trainer of my own and put it to the test. Putting on the plastic headset (complete with metal sensors), I felt like a character in a science fiction movie. When I switched on the machine, a little fan kicked on and hummed quietly while the ping-pong ball sat at the bottom of a foot-long vertical plastic tube. I squinted my eyes and tried to focus on the machine. Suddenly, the fan sprang to life, blowing the ball way up into the tube. Surprised, I lost my focus, and just like that, it dropped back down again. Whoa.

Within fifteen minutes, I was able to move the ball up and down at will, hovering at various heights with at least some measure of control. This was insane. I had mind bullets. It made me wonder what else I could control with my thoughts.

As it turns out, quite a lot. Although the technology behind these headsets is still being developed and fine-tuned, companies like NeuroSky and Emotiv are busy applying this technology to everything from your instant messages (smile and Emotiv's headset will enter a smiley face for you) to hands-free video games that help kids with attention deficit disorder. And that's just the tip of the iceberg. Someday you'll come home and close your garage door simply by thinking: *close.*

On the more practical end of the spectrum, Toyota's Collaboration Center in Japan has developed a wheelchair for victims of paralysis that responds to brain waves. It's the snappiest version of this technology that I've yet seen yet. In their video demonstration a volunteer pilots an equipped chair through a variety of obstacles quickly and easily with nothing but his mind.

The scale and scope of these noninvasive BCI innovations is hardly possible to predict at this point, but I can confidently say that we haven't seen anything yet. When the system *knows* you're bored because it can read your brain waves, you won't have to wait long for things to get interesting. When your employer can track your "focus score" for the week, you'll pay closer attention. Rest assured, wherever feedback can find us, it will. In a world where our brain has become the primary method of controlling the world around us, the games we might play are inconceivable today.

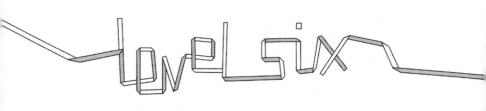

Is this our destiny? Are these visions of the future inevitable? Are they progress? I'm skeptical. And not because I believe that a truly ubiquitous game is implausible. But rather, because I see major hurdles in our way if we plan to use games to influence behavior on a mass scale.

It's easy to follow the logic that will lead us astray: if one game works in getting people to do what we want, why not a hundred? And with so many point systems and incentives out there, why not link them all together? It's already happened for the loyalty programs of airlines, hotels, and credit cards. Expanding to the rest of the world isn't such a stretch.

Yet, I suspect we'll respond very poorly to the kind of "forced" play that will ensue if these kinds of games are promoted as a cultural cure-all. If we encourage people to play games that put corporate priorities ahead of their own, we run the risk of making games become work. And while the serious games used in education or the military can get away with required play, many games can't. Because play, at its core, is an activity that originates in freedom.

Regardless, it's clear that forces are converging that will put games (and the dynamics that make them captivating) in a position to affect our most basic institutions. Game designers will soon find themselves in a most influential position, with the ability to reshape the world around us. What we need most is a responsible shared approach to game design that will help us achieve our potential while retaining our humanity.

So what criticism can be leveled against the notion of a ubiquitous game built purely upon points and incentives? For starters, there is evidence to suggest that we don't respond well to predictable external rewards over the long term. Furthermore, there's no evidence that constant gameplay is something we're equipped to deal with. While our attraction to play is instinctual, our instincts often lead us to overindulge, and such a system could result in mindless or dishonest behavior. Finally, any governing body entrusted to design and manage a game that touches every aspect of our lives would be hopelessly biased toward its own ends. Let's examine these hurdles in more detail.

Rewards Are a Crutch

The simplicity of tangible rewards makes them an easy crutch to fall back on when designing any experience meant to promote specific behavior. Anything you want to encourage you just reward, right? It's true that rewards and prizes are part of why we play games. But they alone don't account for the recipe that makes games effective.

To argue whether positive reinforcement works is to miss the point. Clearly it does work at least some of time—our entire economy is built on a system of currency people earn for their hard work. No, the question isn't *if* rewards work, it's *when*.

One frequently quoted study illustrates the complexities of the subject. In it, three groups of preschoolers were presented with special felt-tipped pens for drawing. One group received no mention of rewards. Another group was promised a special ribbon for drawing with the pens. And the last group received a surprise ribbon only after choosing to draw.

The researchers then studied their behavior in the days after the rewards were given. The kids who received a promised ribbon drew less. The kids who received nothing drew about the same. And the kids who received a surprise ribbon—well, they drew most of all.

It would seem that a strong response to variable reinforcement is built right into us. Indeed, that's why many of the games that require repetitive tasks use variable rewards to encourage those behaviors (slot machines pay out, but only once in a while). Predictable rewards, like a free gift with purchase, simply become expectations. We weave them into our value equation and they lose their ability to engage us.

Turning Play into Work

In cases like the one above, psychologists refer to the phenomenon of demotivation through rewards as the overjustification effect. They suggest that the presence of a stated reward confuses us about *why* we're doing something. It's as if bringing a reward into the mix has the potential to change a naturally intrinsic activity into something that feels extrinsic. Sometimes, rewards can turn play into work. This mental change, once made, is hard to undo.

However, it's important to note that the *kind* of reward really does matter. While we usually conceive of rewards and prizes as *things*—objects with monetary or social value—many other outcomes can be viewed as rewards. Earning the right to make a decision can be a reward. Access to a new experience or opportunity counts too. Any outcome that is desirable to a person can be used as a reward to encourage specific behavior.

According to cognitive evaluation theory, more tangible rewards (money, prizes, and points to some extent) have the potential to be perceived as coercive and controlling. In general, researchers have found that informational rewards like praise or encouragement actually tend to increase our feelings of internal competence and control, and therefore do not have the same detrimental effects. It may be that praise personalizes our accomplishments (feeding our sense of self), while tangible rewards abstract them.

The Right Reasons

The importance of being intrinsically motivated in our activities is evocative of the autotelic personality described in *Flow*. The term *autotelic* can be defined as "doing something for its own sake." Csikszentmihalyi believes that we should be treating each activity as valuable in and of itself, without concern for external validation or reward.

Two other related terms from the work of psychologist Michael Apter help illuminate the merits of rewards: telic and paratelic. Telic simply means goal-oriented: doing something for the outcome. Running errands is telic. Paratelic means moment-oriented: seeking to experience enjoyment in the here and now. A full body massage is paratelic. One way to make sense of the overjustification effect would be to assume that tangible rewards are causing a switch between momentary/paratelic and goal-based/telic states in our minds. So, if players are naturally engaged in an activity, we should be mindful of how we reward them—goals are conducive to engagement and flow, but a focus on rewards *as* goals can lead to hollow experiences.

Your Brain is a Juggler

If you've ever attempted to juggle, you were probably able to get three balls going for a moment or two. If you stuck with it, perhaps you're that guy who can juggle for minutes on end, given a few random objects at a dinner party. And then you have your circus acts—the juggling savants—able to juggle bowling pins and chainsaws. But even among the best jugglers in the world, there is a limit to how long they can keep it up, and it's not forever. An hour of juggling is a lot, and then it's time for a rest.

Your prefrontal cortex, the part of your brain that orchestrates your conscious thoughts and decisions as you move through your day, is like a juggler. It can only handle so much information at any one time, and it can only last for so long.

Games are like objects to juggle. They require focus, attention, and commitment. Whether it be a board game or the latest interactive masterpiece, there's a cognitive investment to be made in just finding your footing within a new system of rules and action. We can play for hours on end, but at some point we need a break—a recharge. In today's world, this isn't a problem, because we choose the games we play and when we play them. But if games were to become truly ubiquitous, the reality of our limits would be exposed, and quickly. Sometimes we simply don't want to play, and while play can absolutely happen instinctually, it doesn't happen against our will.

Grinding it Out

Some people believe that a ubiquitous game would lead to what gamers call "grinding." In video games, grinding simply means performing repetitive or boring tasks in order to earn access to features or levels within the game. Killing the same monster over and over again in *Final Fantasy XI* becomes increasingly less rewarding, but if it offers an easy way to level up, many players will suffer through it. In a points-based ubiquitous game, it's possible that people would see almost *every* activity as a grind—something that they'd do repeatedly just to get the points.

Although incentives can encourage specific behavior, players in this situation may bypass the act of learning *why* an activity is important or valuable. In a ubiquitous game, will you read a book for enjoyment, or just because you want the points? On Gamasutra.com, discussing this same topic, Ian Bogost tells us why the thought behind our actions matters: ". . . to thrive, culture requires deliberation and rationale in addition to convention. When we think about what to do in a given situation, we may fall back on actions which come easily or have incentives attached to them. But when we consider which situations themselves are more or less important, we must make appeals to a higher order." Basically, we can't rely on points alone to tell us which activities are important, or *we risk losing our sense of self to a leaderboard.*

Of course, anywhere that a grind exists—where repetitive work can yield rewards—you'll find people *gaming the system*. The system says to them, "It's all about the rewards," and so that's exactly what they pursue, and by any means necessary. Ask any game designer with a popular game on the market and they'll tell you—people find ways to cut corners.

In a ubiquitous game where behaviors have a point value that corporations and governments are willing to pay for, enterprising people will inevitably find ways to take advantage. If your shoes give you points for walking, then why not invent a little contraption that walks your shoes? We can't even imagine the hacks that emerge from a system like this, but I can assure you, wherever a high points to activity ratio exists, you'll find unsportsmanlike conduct.

Who's Behind the Curtain?

One common concern in turning all of culture into a game is this: who makes the rules? Because our behavior is so valuable to corporations, it's easy to see how their ambitions would dominate a ubiquitous game. But there are also governments, nonprofits, and religion to consider. After all, everyone has something to gain from influencing our choices, right? How could we possibly decide who gets to make the call?

Even something as simple as how long we should be brushing our teeth is difficult. Is it Oral B's decision, if they're footing the bill? Or do we leave that to the American Dental Association? And what about your dentist's opinion on the matter? What happens if your teeth are particularly sensitive?

Above all, we have to recognize that corporate agendas seldom align with our own best interest. Does a bookstore really care if you finish reading a book? Or if you grokked it? They simply want you to buy another one. Whoever pays for the rewards in a system like this will decide what matters, and the noble notion of personal development that excites so many of us is not a well-funded aspiration.

If we want to use games to reach our true potential, we're going to have to approach them with more than points, rewards, and ubiquity. Lucky for us, there are many people out there thinking about how to influence behavior for the common good. But to appreciate them, we're going to have to take a step back.

How the World Works

Let's say you want your kid to take out the trash. How would you go about encouraging this? If you're like most people, you'd probably offer her something in return: "Take out the garbage and you'll get a weekly allowance." If that doesn't work, you might break out the trusty old threat of punishment: "If you don't take out the trash, you're grounded."

This approach works reasonably well, right? It must, because it is the primary mechanism behind civilized society. Work hard, and you can buy a big house. Break the rules, and you're off to the "Big House."

Where Did We Get That Idea?

In the early 1900s psychologist Edward Thorndike began a series of experiments with cats that shaped our thinking on the psychology of learning. In these tests, he put cats into a maze-like puzzle box and studied them as they figured out an escape route. He posited that as the cats made choices leading to their escape (a positive outcome), that path became associated with positive feelings of freedom. When they made choices that led to continued entrapment, their frustration and angst were associated with those bad choices. Over several trials in the box, these associations helped the cats learn how to get out quickly. With this simple model, Thorndike was able to create some of the very first learning curves, and the field of operant conditioning was born.

Operant Conditioning

Operant conditioning was later evolved to greater levels of specificity and control by a psychologist named B. F. Skinner. Skinner was one of the early proponents of behaviorism, a learning theory suggesting that psychology should be explored only through observable behavior and conditioning. His work on operant conditioning included concepts like reinforcement, punishment, and extinction (eliminating the unintentional reinforcement of a bad behavior). Reinforcement and punishment can each be enforced in two different ways: positive, which means something is added to the situation; or negative, which means something is taken away. Those variables result in four kinds of consequences to behavior. Let's apply them to our earlier example of taking out the trash:

> ‣ Positive reinforcement: an allowance
> ‣ Negative reinforcement: letting her skip another chore
> ‣ Positive punishment: adding more chores to her list
> ‣ Negative punishment: taking away her favorite snacks

Today, these consequences remain very popular in our government, educational systems, and workplace. Equally interesting in the context of games are the factors that behaviorists have determined alter the *effectiveness* of the consequences above:

> ‣ Satiation/deprivation: how recently an individual has been satiated by a particular reward will affect how compelling it is. If you've just had a milkshake, you're going to be a lot less willing to work for another one. But, if you've been deprived of sweets, the presence of a milkshake will be quite enticing.
> ‣ Immediacy: how soon a reward is offered after a desired behavior will strengthen or weaken the conditioning. Waiting until the end of the semester to reward students for good grades doesn't do much to motivate them on the first day of school.
> ‣ Contingency: how reliably a reward is given affects the speed

and permanence of a learned behavior. More consistent rewards lead to rapid learning but also faster abandonment when the rewards stop.

> Size: how sizable or valuable a reward is will impact the strength of the response to it. Who doesn't want a bigger bonus, bigger house, or bigger lottery jackpot?

Although operant conditioning and behaviorism offer much in terms of a framework for learning and influencing behavior, they have been largely discredited as oversimplifications. They ignore the complex mental states that influence and drive external behavior—behavior that is often difficult to explain or predict. Today, psychologists draw from a complex body of knowledge that combines the best of both worlds: our internal thought processes as well as our external triggers. But it's our thought processes that can be most puzzling.

The Science of Irrationality

While behaviorism is all about individuals doing what is *expected* to gain rewards and avoid punishment, the field of behavioral economics is all about the *unexpected*. In the early days of economic theory, it was widely believed that people made choices in order to maximize utility—to get the most value for their time, money, or energy. In essence, it was suggested that humans were perfectly rational beings when it came to economic choices. As anyone who has spent even a minute watching the stock market can tell you, this is patently false.

In the late 1960s and early 1970s several researchers, including Daniel Kahneman, Amos Tversky, Gary Becker, and Herbert Simon began releasing papers and studies which indicated that in a wide variety of circumstances, people were surprisingly irrational decision makers.

In one experiment, some participants were given a nice coffee mug while others were not. Then, both groups were asked to value the mug. The people who had been given a mug of their own believed it was more valuable than participants who did not receive one. This phenomenon, known as the endowment effect, states that we ascribe inflated value to things that we already have in our possession. This goes against traditional economic theory of course, where a $1.50 mug should hold the same value to us whether we're buying it or selling it. As it turns out, there are hundreds of examples of this kind of illogical behavior, known to economists and psychologists as cognitive biases.

Once you accept that many of our decisions and actions are clouded by irrationality, one major question comes to mind: how can we use this information to help people make better decisions? A few prominent behavioral economists believe that we simply need a nudge in the right direction.

What's a Nudge?

Several popular books on the subject of behavioral economics have come out in the last few years, most notably *Predictably Irrational* by Dan Ariely and *Nudge* by Richard Thaler and Cass Sunstein. *Nudge* is particularly intriguing, since it takes a very prescriptive approach to the subject matter. In it, Thaler and Sunstein explain that for every choice we make, certain forces in our environment and context play a role in shaping that decision.

Consider the form we complete to get a driver's license, specifically the question about organ donation. If the goal is to maximize donations, should the form ask us to check a box *to* donate, or to check a box if we *don't want* to donate? It turns out that something as insignificant as the phrasing of a question actually makes a huge difference, even with something as serious as our organs. This is due to the status quo bias, which states that we have an innate preference for going along with present circumstances.

Throughout the text, the authors refer to the manipulation of these circumstances as "choice architecture." Thaler and Sunstein assert that each of us has the potential to be a choice architect—a position of great power—as we choose the context in which our citizens, employees, and children will make decisions.

We have the power to nudge people into doing the right thing. Sound a bit too controlling? They don't think so. The authors even coined the term "libertarian paternalism" to describe their philosophy: libertarian because they believe in the freedom to choose, and paternalism because they believe that no choice is free of external influence, and so we have a duty to help everyone make better decisions.

Throughout *Nudge*, the authors make reference to several factors that could just as easily be discussed during a class on game design. Most notably, they discuss feedback and the role of organized and clear information in the midst of difficult decisions. Many of the situations discussed in the book pivot on time, social pressure, and competition—all elements used in modern game design.

While the relatively new field of behavioral economics does have its similarities to game design in terms of influencing behavior, there are also marked differences. *Nudge* mostly deals with complex choices that have long-term consequences. In contrast, game design is usually focused on momentary choices that result in near-term feedback and results—play that's happening now.

Additionally, in the world of *Nudge*, it's the choices that matter, not the experience of making them. The authors do not go into great detail about the cognitive experience of the people filling out organ donation forms, because most of the influence is happening at a very subconscious level. In a game designed to affect behavior, however, the *experience* of making choices and taking action is paramount. Rather than simply influencing choices, games can make the experience of any activity richer and more fulfilling by making it fun.

The Fun Theory

One glimpse of fun in action can be found in Stockholm, Sweden. In late 2009, Volkswagen and DDB Stockholm partnered on a new initiative they called The Fun Theory, a program with the following mission statement: "Fun is the easiest way to change people's behavior for the better." I couldn't agree more.

The goal of this clever contest was to solicit ideas from the general public demonstrating how fun could change behavior for the common good. These ideas might help to protect the environment, improve public health, or make the city more beautiful. The common denominator was that every idea should make things better, as defined by the participants. Submitted ideas were to be reviewed by a panel of experts and the winner awarded 2,500 euros.

In order to inspire participants and get some attention for the program, the DDB team took to the streets of Stockholm and tested several wild theories of their own, the most popular being an experiment called Piano Staircase. At the mouth of a popular subway stop, travelers were faced with a choice: take the stairs or the escalator. Not surprisingly, the vast majority typically chose the less healthy option: the escalator. The Fun Theory team wondered if they could change that.

Under cover of darkness, the team quickly outfitted the stairs with an array of sensors and audio equipment that made each stair emit a musical tone. To make it even more fun, they colored the steps to look like piano keys.

The next morning, the team let their hidden cameras roll and waited to see what would happen. The results were staggering: 66 percent more people took the stairs, and what's more, they seemed to genuinely enjoy doing it. The team quickly posted a video of their experiment on YouTube. It's since been viewed by millions around the globe.

Another of The Fun Theory's popular ideas was dubbed Bottle Bank Arcade. In Sweden, the recycle bins that live on city streets are called bottle banks. They're large green bins with a horizontal row of circular holes at the top. The hope is that pedestrians will drop their used bottles and cans into these receptacles rather than the garbage. Unfortunately, this doesn't always happen. Again, The Fun Theory team sprang into action with a solution.

They added a score board to the top of a standard bin, and wired the deposit holes with sensors and lights. This new bin would challenge players to drop bottles into *specific* holes only when they were illuminated (a clever reversal of the familiar arcade game of Whac-A-Mole). The bin also kept track of a high score, so passersby could compete.

That evening, the "improved" bin saw over one hundred people use it, while another nearby bin was used only twice. Younger players were literally hunting down more bottles and cans just for the chance to play again.

Overall, The Fun Theory site collected hundreds of entries suggesting a myriad of ways to add some fun back into our lives and improve the world in the process. Given the scope of the issues we're facing today, we could use a locally funded version of this initiative in *every* community.

Games Won't Save Us, but Their Ingredients Might

Having just explored current thinking on how games, play, rewards, nudges, and fun motivate us and shape our actions, it becomes clear that it's not games themselves, but their fundamental building blocks—their ingredients—that awaken something primal within us. Knowing that we might go too far with games, I see these ingredients as an alternate course. If living in a world that feels like a game sounds attractive, it's because each of us believes that games are more inspiring, more exciting, and more equitable than reality. If we can become experts at applying game dynamics to our own lives—our offices, our schools, and our homes—then we can realize the benefits of games without waiting for a ubiquitous solution. This notion of applied games—designed to help us engage and achieve in our real lives—is something we've been playing at since the beginning, but without a way to frame the discussion. That's all about to change.

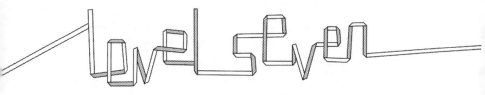

If you're Nike, running is good for business. Which means you're faced with three goals: get more people running, get them running more often, and (while you're at it) get them to run farther. How in the hell do you do that? You could spend a fortune on celebrity endorsements, marketing, or distribution, as Nike clearly does. But that will only *sell* the shoes, it won't wear them out. No, what you do—if you want to achieve all of these goals—is invent Nike+.

Already well publicized over the last several years, Nike+ is a marvel of the digital age, not for its technical complexity, but for its impact on casual runners. Created in partnership with Apple, the system requires three major components: a shoe sensor, an iPod, and the Nike+ website.

The sensor, a small accelerometer about the size of a quarter, drops into your favorite pair of Nikes, and measures your speed and distance as you run. Your iPod receives this information wirelessly and uses it to report your performance, motivate you with a peppy song or some words of encouragement, and keep you informed on your overall progress.

When you return from your run and sync your iPod, the Nike+ website presents you with a rich visualization of your workout. It also shares data from your run with your friends, family, and other members of the running community, and updates your overall running history.

The entire suite of Nike+ products has been wildly popular. Over 1 million runners use it, making it the world's largest running club. Together, they've logged over 275 million miles. Undoubtedly, some of this popularity results from a low barrier to entry. After all, the sensor is only $29 and the vast majority of runners already have an iPod. However, the product's solid reputation comes from the fact that it gives runners motivation and social support that they can't seem to get anywhere else.

Why Nike+ Works

The Nike+ system works because it offers runners a few unique benefits. First, and most important, Nike+ offers both real-time and post-run feedback. "How fast am I running? How far have I gone? Am I doing better than last week?" In the past, this kind of motivational feedback has been largely unavailable to runners, and certainly not in such a user-friendly package.

In addition to feedback, the system offers social pressure in the form of an active online community. As a member, you can choose personal goals and share them with your friends, family, and other Nike+ users. As you make progress, they hear about it and get to cheer you on.

Finally, the Nike+ website offers competition. Runners compete against friends, running partners, and other opponents. The system offers advanced sorting features allowing many different levels of rivalry (neighborhoods can compete against other neighborhoods for instance). Nike also holds community-wide events such as the annual Nike+ Human Race—a 10k race in more than twenty-five cities that is purported to be the world's largest one-day running event. All of these elements add up to an incredibly sticky system, one that motivates and engages people of all ages and skill levels.

Amidst all the accolades directed at the product line, many people have noticed that Nike+ is more than just a performance-enhancing technology. It's also a game. Runners aren't simply using Nike+; they're playing it. For some, this manifests in more joyful running, because the feedback from the system encourages their goals and tracks progress. For others, the prestige of the online leaderboard triggers their competitive drive, and they strive to move up in the standings.

These are behaviors we're used to seeing among gamers, but it's a bit odd to see them in casual runners. After all, running isn't really a game—it's primarily a form of exercise. These are real runners on *real runs*. Yet undeniably, there is a certain element of play at work here, and it's this dynamic that is at the heart of the product's success. With Nike+, the line between reality and games is being blurred, and as a result, running is a more entertaining and satisfying experience. Meanwhile, Nike shoes all over the world are getting one heck of a workout.

For Love of Meta

If running can be made more engaging and even fun, then why not everything else? Can we reshape the world around us to be *more like a game*, without falling victim to the challenges facing ubiquitous gaming? The answer lies in an unexpected place: a notion of conceptual layering known as *meta*.

Meta is an old Greek prefix that simply means an abstraction of another concept. Metadata, for example, is data about other data. The Dewey decimal system is metadata (authors, titles, locations) about a library's books, which themselves are filled with data and information. Meta-advertising, on the other hand, is advertising that promotes other ads, as we sometimes see in the days leading up to the Super Bowl.

Lots of creative and conversational energy goes into meta activities these days, because abstraction is actually quite an addictive psychological behavior. It's surprisingly easy, for example, to find yourself commenting on a blog post *about* commenting on blog posts.

Our brains enjoy this thought process because abstraction is one way that we manage all the complexity we encounter in the world. It allows us to relate the concrete world (the book you're holding) to philosophical concepts (the idea of "books"). And it's this ability to categorize and relate ideas to objects with great sophistication that really sets us apart as a species. Naturally, then, exploring the meta is quite popular across a multitude of activities, including gaming.

In keeping with our earlier examples, a *metagame* is a game that happens on top of—or inside of—another game. This involves using information or expectations from outside the game itself, ultimately affecting in-game behavior. *Speed runs*, the act of trying to beat a video game as quickly as possible, are a common example of a metagame. In this case, the player has created a race within a gaming environment that was not designed to be time sensitive. In an action adventure game, a player might choose to pretend that he has only one life—ceasing to play when he is killed—even though the game allows restarting at any time. Metagames are our way of making gameplay more interesting and more personal.

In *Open*, Andre Agassi's autobiography, he describes how his father made him hit 2,500 balls a day at the age of seven, for a total of *one million balls a year*. As part of this grueling process, young Agassi reimagined the ball machine as a black dragon, spitting balls in an attempt to smite him. In terms of meta, this is fascinating. The game of tennis, turned into work through sheer intensity, and then back into a game: Agassi versus the dragon.

The Game Layer

Online community expert and game designer Amy Jo Kim sees many of the habitual behaviors happening on the web—people collecting followers on Twitter or working to improve their eBay reputation score—as a class of metagames. These mechanisms seem as important to their users as the services themselves. Many recently popular websites and mobile applications have begun to leverage game mechanics in this way, in order to increase engagement and loyalty.

Of course, there's a fundamental problem with using the

same nomenclature for these sites and services that we use in the world of gaming. Strictly speaking, these activities *aren't actually metagames*. Why not? Because they're not played on top of *games* . . . they're played on top of *websites*.

Playing games on top of other experiences comes so naturally to us that we make up new ways to do it all the time. Ever avoid stepping on cracks as you walked home? Ever stand in line for concessions at the movies and have a friend stand in another, just to see who will get there first? Or perhaps while working out, you've fantasized that the safety of the world depends on completing that last quarter mile. These mental gymnastics happen effortlessly, and they spice things up.

This phenomenon isn't limited to our spare time either. It's quite common to hear top performers in any field talk about their day-to-day work in terms of play. The physicist P.A.M. Dirac once described his early days as a physicist in a way that most people would not associate with quantum physics, "It was a good description to say that it was a game, a very interesting game one could play."

If these games we're playing with ourselves are not metagames in the strictest sense of the word, what are they? They're *a game layer* thrown over our lives—a natural manifestation of our playful disposition. And while some of these games are nonsensical, many serve a loftier purpose: to combat our lack of volition and faculty. When designed with intent, I refer to them as *behavioral games*.

A behavioral game is a real world activity modified by a system of skills-based play.

Where behavioral games differ from traditional games is in the psychological space of the gameplay itself. While almost every other game unfolds in some kind of magic circle, behavioral games unfold in our offices, schools, and homes. Further, while commercial games are most often focused on mass market appeal, many behavioral games have an audience of just one, allowing these systems to be incredibly bespoke.

Behavioral games matter because they have the power to make almost any activity more engaging and conducive to learning. They accomplish this by applying the dynamics of games to everyday experiences. To better understand the concept, let's look at an example of a behavioral game from an organization with over a century of experience motivating its members.

Nearly one hundred years ago, the Boy Scouts of America began offering merit badges for mastering certain survival skills, including carpentry, pathfinding, signaling, and tracking. These simple tokens turned learning complex new skills into an acquisitive experience and a form of public achievement. Today, there are well over one hundred individual badges that can be earned for skills ranging from space exploration to stamp collecting.

Being a Boy Scout is ultimately about learning to survive in the wild. Yet, collecting merit badges and earning new ranks makes that process far more structured and enjoyable. The merit badge system is built on top of a survival curriculum to facilitate learning and development, which puts substance behind it, making it far more valuable than compulsive collecting. It's an excellent example of a behavioral game that has worked for generations.

Just like the Boy Scouts, we have the opportunity to design behavioral games that will unfold in our everyday lives and improve our experience. They represent a powerful cure to our lack of faculty and volition.

Potential for Play

So, what sorts of activities can we turn into behavioral games? Daniel Cook, game designer and co-founder of game development studio Spry Fox, has proposed a sound method for evaluating the potential for play. Any activity can be turned into a game:

> If the activity can be learned,
> If the player can be measured, and
> If the play can be rewarded or punished in a timely fashion.

Behavioral games focus on skills that matter to the activity at hand. Few things are more frustrating than practicing a skill without a place to use it. That's why "When am I ever going to use this?" is such a common complaint in classrooms across the globe. Without purpose, random skills and knowledge seem meaningless. In behavioral games, what we do, and how we do it, affects our experience. A behavioral game is perfectly practical about skills. We use them to play, and we need to improve them to win.

Daniel Cook has written extensively about taking a skills-based approach to understanding a player's experience *in a game* rather than just *of a game*. According to him, players are people driven to learn new skills that are high in perceived value. In this way, we're all basically "skill chasers." To elaborate, he puts forth the idea of a "skill atom," which is essentially a simple feedback loop within a game. Players digest that feedback and use it to update their understanding of the system. If their action netted positive results, they'll likely feel good. If it didn't, they may become bored or frustrated. Skill atoms can be looped over and over again until a player groks the skill in question.

Games link these skill atoms together to form more and more complicated "skill chains." For example, accelerating in a car is a skill atom, but combining it with braking, turning, and avoiding other cars creates a skill chain that allows a driver to get around the racetrack.

One subset of skills quite pertinent to behavioral games are skills that have been burned out, meaning that a player is no longer interested in using them. This represents much of what we do on a day-to-day basis in our jobs and homes. Emptying the dishwasher is essentially a burned-out skill. Behavioral games force us to observe this behavior and create solutions. Are people losing interest in certain skills? Are they having trouble seeing how two skill atoms fit together to make a more valuable skill chain? As we look at our lives and the network of skills that we're using, we too need to identify those gaps and find lasting solutions.

Considerations

Based on current trends, it would be fair to assume that the most effective behavioral games will be tethered to our consoles, computers, and mobile phones. After all, we're a digital culture now. However, it's important to recognize that the concept of behavioral games was alive long before the invention of the microprocessor. For every example like Nike+ there's an analog instance like the Boy Scouts. We simply have to choose the best tools for the job.

Behavioral games also give us a new way to evaluate the quality and merit of our experiences. They change the nature of our activities by showing us where to focus our attention. As we begin to learn what is important and relevant, our senses pick up on subtleties that would have eluded us previously. A master sommelier for instance, is able to detect flavors in wine that the average person cannot. Why? Because she has refined her skill at this task through repetition and focus. To her, the tasting is a puzzle game—one in which the flavors are the clues to a larger story. By telling us what to focus on, behavioral games give us a new perspective.

Of course, like any game, some behavioral games are deep, and others are shallow. The truth is that not all game mechanics are created equal. Every game has its *core mechanic*—the main mechanism for play. Recalling *Super Mario Brothers* once more, it's the running and jumping that are core to the game. Everything else—the points, stars, and mushrooms—is secondary. In the world of behavioral games, *deep* engagement comes from finding the best mechanism for play within the activity. Shallow behavioral games simply rely on game mechanics that are popular and easy to implement.

It may be that some of the most popular game mechanics are actually a bit meta in their own right, since they often only matter outside the activity (i.e., points that do nothing but feed a leaderboard). The downside of the recent popularity of mechanics like points and badges is that the world is falling in love with them in isolation, and missing the boat on the dynamics of learning and skills acquisition that make behavioral games really special.

Becoming Designers

Grokking the systems that define our lives is the great task of all behavioral games. Good behavioral games, then, should reveal something fundamental about the underlying activities they're built around. Achieving this requires examining the structure of our own activities and experiences in more depth than ever before. This process of observation and inquiry is the precursor to design. Indeed, to reshape the world around us—our workplace, our schools, our homes—we must become behavioral game *designers*.

A behavioral game is made up of ten building blocks. Together, they comprise a design framework that I call the Game Frame. To begin the process of designing behavioral games, we first have to understand the components that make them up. Like traditional games, behavioral games have many interrelated pieces that add up to an engaging experience. In this way, our design framework is no different from that of any other game designer. Using a Game Frame allows us to look at any behavioral game from the top down, understand its constituent parts, and see how they fit together.

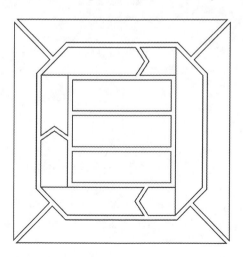

Activity

The *activity* in a behavioral game is the real-world endeavor that the game is built upon. Identifying an activity is as simple as finding an area of focus—something we want players to do more, better, or differently. Some good examples of activities include studying, exercising, cooking, painting, brainstorming, relaxing, and so on. Activities are verbs. They are the things we do.

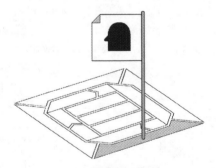

Player Profile

The *player profile* is a trait-based description of the players in a behavioral game. Since we're attempting to influence *specific* players, the player profile offers us the information we need in the form of two key variables: drivers and symptoms.

Drivers are psychological traits that help us understand

which dynamics will motivate our players. Based in part on existing models of personality, I have identified four dyads against which I evaluate players. Each one represents a continuum between two drivers that can increase or decrease volition and faculty. For the player profile we need to determine (by observation or inquiry) which end of the spectrum motivates our players most.

ACHIEVEMENT of goals | ENJOYMENT of experience
STRUCTURE and guidance | FREEDOM to explore
CONTROL of others | ACCEPTANCE of others
SELF-INTEREST in actions | SOCIAL INTEREST in actions

Achievement versus enjoyment gets at the heart of how players evaluate an experience. Is it the outcome or the process that matters to them?

Structure versus freedom tells us something about their learning style. Do they want to master skills through instruction, or to figure things out for themselves?

Control versus acceptance indicates how they define power. Do they get it from dominion over others, or from their connection to community?

Self-interest versus social interest gives us clues about their idea of success. Is it about their *own* progression, or overall progress?

Every player has a tendency toward one end of each dyad, and that tendency can inform the kind of dynamics we create in our behavioral games. For instance, a player who prefers achievement and structure will probably respond quite well to a competition with strict rules. The connection between drivers and dynamics is subtle, but I suspect you'll find value in considering them as you design the building blocks of your games.

The other half of a player profile, the symptoms, are the now quite familiar topics of volition and faculty. A complete player profile will indicate whether one or both of these is a possible issue and how they are manifesting themselves, allowing us to design accordingly. For example, a player low in faculty may appreciate a behavioral game with clear instructions and levels.

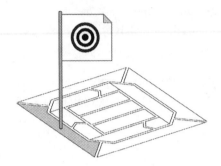

Objectives

Objectives are goals toward which effort is directed. There are two kinds of objectives in a behavioral game: short-term and long-term. A long-term goal is the ultimate objective. It's how we determine if and when the game has been won. Without a long-term goal, it would be unclear what we are trying to accomplish. Short-term goals are the things that must be accomplished along the way. In a complex game, they focus our efforts and give us a clear indication of what to do next. Success in short-term goals is both rewarding and motivating, and afterward players look confidently to the next challenge. In many cases where a behavioral game is required, short-term and long-term objectives are not presently clear, and need to be made up altogether. A sound long-term goal should be an end state desired by everyone involved: the players *and* the system in which they're playing. Beyond that, long-term goals have the potential to give players narrative context. If the ultimate objective is to put the competition out of business, then everything we do is in service of that rivalry.

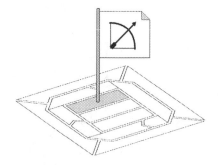

Skills

Skills are specialized abilities that we put to use in behavioral games. By definition, skills are abilities that we can learn, and learning new skills is one of the most satisfying things that players can do. You can see the delight in a child's eyes when he masters a new skill—riding a bike for instance—and it's no different with adults, we just tend to forget that there are new skills out there waiting for us. Skills come in many variations, but are easily divided into three categories: physical skills (like skiing, running, or using a chef's knife), mental skills (such as pattern recognition, memory, spatial logic, and organization), and social skills (like presentation, conversation, and meeting new people). Behavioral game design requires that we're conscious of all three, and develop our chosen skills through play. What's more, behavioral game design ensures that the skills we develop in a game are useful and practical within the game itself—that in essence, improving our abilities unlocks features or experiences that we desire.

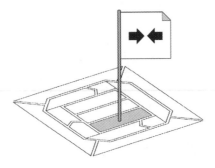

Resistance

Resistance is the force of opposition that creates tension in a behavioral game. One of the most counterintuitive things about games is that players don't like a sure thing. Playing a game we know we're going to win is no fun. To understand why, we have to recall that games are learning engines—not just pastimes—so what we expect from them above all is a chance to learn. Learning, by definition, is about growth. We grow by stretching our body and mind. If a game is guaranteed to go our way, then we don't need to stretch. We can simply watch things unfold. So then, behavioral games require some element of uncertainty to be engaging and to deliver on their promise. That uncertainty comes in many shapes and sizes, and is most aptly described as resistance. Two common forms of resistance are competition and chance. Competition pits players against one another, and chance subjects players to unpredictable circumstances. Every behavioral game has some form of resistance, and many variations of this important building block exist.

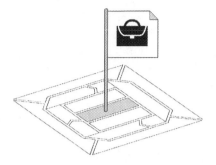

Resources

Resources are the spaces and supplies that players use, or have the potential to acquire, in behavioral games. Traditional games often require material goods and spaces: pieces, cards, boards, courts, balls, ammunition, and anything else required to play. Each of these objects has specific attributes (what it can do and what can be done with it) and states (i.e., active/inactive). For our purposes, I've grouped all these necessary elements into the building block of resources. In a behavioral game focused on cooking, for instance, resources might include a kitchen, kitchen utensils, a selection of ingredients, and recipe cards.

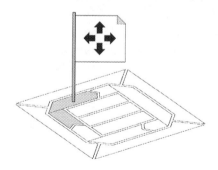

Actions

Actions are the moves available to players in a behavioral game. This includes what they are allowed to do as well as the when,

93

where, and how of those moves. Importantly, actions are inclusive of decisions and choices. In some games, simply making decisions is enough to propel the game along. In others, more active play is required. Actions are typically additive (i.e., do more work), while decisions can be additive *or* negative (i.e., decide to start or stop eating junk food). Actions influence the tone and style of a behavioral game, so we must choose them carefully.

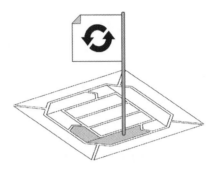

Feedback

Feedback is a system response to a player's actions. Feedback comes in many different forms, ranging from data and information (such as a speedometer) to auditory stimulation (such as a room full of laughter). Without feedback, it would be completely unclear what effect (if any) our actions are having in a behavioral game. In this way, feedback is one of the broadest building blocks, representing every mechanism that can react to a player. Because feedback is our main method of evaluating our performance, it has a strong relationship with our sense of faculty—if we're getting good feedback, we become more confident that we can achieve our objectives. Feedback can impact our sense of volition as well. If we experience a pattern of positive feedback, we often feel more motivated to continue. The feedback loop is a fundamental element in learning and making sense of the world around us.

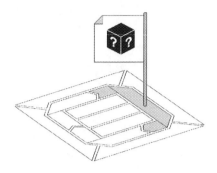

Black Box

The *black box* is a rules engine within a behavioral game. Because behavioral games come in many forms, the black box could be a computer program or a document, or reside in the game designer's head. The important thing is that it contains all the information about the interplay between actions and feedback—a record of all possible if/then scenarios. The written instructions that come with a board game are a good example of this concept. In some behavioral games, the black box could be as simple as a few simple rules, in others, it could require serious technology. The Nike+ system illustrates the interplay between actions, feedback, and the black box nicely. In that system, the runner takes *action* by running at a certain pace. The system has the ability to provide *feedback* in the form of auditory encouragement, but the *black box* determines when it will actually play this audio.

Outcomes

Outcomes are positive and negative results that occur while in pursuit of the ultimate objective in a behavioral game. Positive outcomes include tangible and intangible rewards such as moving up a level, while negative outcomes might be starting over or losing key resources. Outcomes are an important culmination of the more immediate feedback players have received, and mark a moment of reflection in any behavioral game.

How They All Fit Together

Now that we've examined the building blocks that make behavioral games work, it's important to understand how they fit together in the Game Frame. The best behavioral games will link these elements together effortlessly, creating a tapestry of experience that motivates, encourages, challenges, and rewards their players. To see how they all work together in unison, let's look at an example from the world of music.

TheSixtyOne.com

One elegant example of the Game Frame can be found on a music website called TheSixtyOne. TheSixtyOne, while not built with this process in mind, is a behavioral game focused on one central *activity*: listening to music. The *player profile* shows hints of volition issues—many consumers are unwilling to do the work required to find an independent artist they really like. In response to this tendency, the *objectives* of the game are to become the ultimate curator (long-term) and to find great new bands on the site (short-term). The *skills* involved include critical listening and predicting what will be popular in the future. The site offers *actions* in the form of small quests like "Listen to seven songs," or "Watch the segment on TheSixtyOne on G4TV." These quests, along with other activities like logging in, earn you a *resource* called "hearts" that can be used to vote for songs. If the songs you vote for become popular, the site gives you *feedback* in the form of email notifications alerting you to their success. The site creates *resistance* by making hearts generally scarce, and limiting your playlist options to one song at a time. The system is a web application that contains its *black box* in the form of code. The *outcomes* of this activity are the many wonderful artists and songs that users discover. All this adds up to a system of reinforcement that makes listening to music a much more focused and enjoyable activity where every song counts.

How to Design Behavioral Games

With those building blocks under our belt, the process of designing a behavioral game is fairly straightforward. Ensuring that it is engaging, fluid, and stands the test of time however, will require a healthy amount of practice and a willingness to experiment.

In this section, I'll share with you an order of operations for behavioral game design, instructions for each step in the process, and some thought-starters that will increase your chances of success. To make these steps more tangible, we'll walk through the process by focusing on a common problem: a fictional teenager is neglecting to study every day, and when pushed, is having difficulty focusing.

Step One: Choose the Activity

Because we're focusing on practical applications of a game layer in our everyday lives, every behavioral game starts with an activity. The behavior you're trying to create is almost certainly related to an activity. Your job is to select that activity and design a game that will make it better. Remember, with behavioral games, it's not what your players do, but how they do it.

In the case of our fictional student, the activity we're designing for is *studying*.

Tips + Tricks

> Is a behavioral game really the best solution to your problem? If there is an easier or more direct way to tackle your issue, do it.

> Can the skills required by the activity be learned? If not, then a behavioral game won't help.

> Does the activity have the potential for long-term engagement? Are there professionals or "masters" in this field? The presence of experts indicates an area with plenty of room for growth.

> Find the fun. What aspects of the activity are inherently enjoyable when it's done right? Note these aspects now, so you can amplify them later.

> Find the boring. What aspects of the activity are inherently dull? Note these aspects as well, so you can work around them later.

Step Two: Create the Player Profile

To create a player profile, you need to get to know your players. You can do this in any number of ways. Sometimes it makes sense to survey them and get their personal perspective. Other times, observation is enough. Interviewing the people they spend time with can also be extremely informative. At the end of the day, you need to be able to answer two fundamental questions: First, what is holding your player from achieving their potential? Is it the aforementioned lock of faculty or volition? Second, what are the drivers that motivate them?

ACHIEVEMENT of goals | **ENJOYMENT** of the experience
STRUCTURE and guidance | **FREEDOM** to explore
CONTROL of others | **ACCEPTANCE** of others
SELF-INTEREST in actions | **SOCIAL INTEREST** in actions

In the case of our student we'll pretend that he is reporting issues of volition; that is, he doesn't really want to study because he finds it boring. We'll also pretend that her drivers are enjoyment, freedom, control, and self-interest. Based on this profile, it's likely that studying feels like an intrusion on her sense of freedom and enjoyment, a loss of control when she is forced to do it, and not in her self-interest (at least in the short term). In later steps, we'll make use of these insights.

Tips + Tricks

> Study your players' behavior during the activity itself. What do they do naturally? Which ends of the dyads do they seem drawn to? What do they pull away from?

> If you happen to be designing a behavioral game for yourself, you can develop your player profile through self-report, but you'll get better results with honest input from friends, family, and colleagues.

> When designing for a large group, such as an office or a university campus, assume that player profiles will map to a bell curve and focus on creating more broadly desirable game dynamics.

Step Three: Choose the Objectives

Remember the idea of the hero's journey? The objectives of a behavioral game are, in many ways, the basis of that quest. First off, your long-term goal must be compelling. Look at your activity and player profile, and consider the different sorts of ultimate objectives that might work. Remember, this could be the mastery of a skill, a new habit, an achievement, a title, or any other pinnacle of personal growth. Next, consider the short-term goals—the steps along the way. What must your players accomplish in order to reach the ultimate objective? How can you break the journey up into discrete and satisfying challenges that push your players and help them improve?

In the case of our student, who is learning the art of studying, possible long-term goals include particular grades in her coursework, a habit of daily study for a certain number of consecutive days, or the ability to retain a certain amount of information after any study session. In a behavioral game, though, it's important to frame things in heroic or aspirational terms. So in this case, we'll invent a new title for our student to strive for: master of studies. A master of studies is a status-based objective with two criteria: fifty consecutive days of studying, while maintaining a grade point average of 3.0 or higher. We'll also want to challenge our student with a short-term goal though, and we'll start with something simple: a minimum number of study hours each week.

Tips + Tricks

> Behavioral games work best when the objectives align with the desires of the players. Find something that they want to accomplish and can get excited about.

> Remember that the ultimate objective should be fairly difficult to achieve—the learning curve required should be steep. Otherwise, you'll be designing the sequel sooner than you'd like.

> Don't go with uninspired objectives just because they describe the outcomes you seek. Figure out a way to make long-term and short-term goals as exciting and aspirational as possible, given your constraints. Go for the glory.

Step Four: Choose the Skill(s)

Skills are the heart of any behavioral game, and they are improved through its play. To define the skills that will be the basis of a behavioral game, consider what abilities are necessary to succeed in the endeavor. The activity and the objectives are a good place to start. Make a skills list, including anything you can think of that is relevant to your game across all three categories of skills: physical, mental, and social. Examples of skills include prediction, survival, collecting, curating, pattern recognition, endurance, time management, trading, racing, and literally thousands of others. An interesting subset is *twitch* skills, which are very common in games. These include any reflex-driven activity, from skeet shooting to trivia. A simple behavioral game might be based on only one core skill, while the activity itself involves several other skills that are not measured within the game. This is okay. Your design determines what skills are the focus. A more complex behavioral game may include three or more skills. Remember, though, the more skills you include, the more complex your design will have to be to accommodate them.

In the case of our student, we'll concentrate on two skills in particular: time management and focus. Time management is an important skill because our student needs to remember to make time for studying or no studying can occur. This then becomes a precursor to any other skill in our game. Focus will be our second skill, because the homework itself is outside our control, making our student's ability to apply herself without distraction paramount.

Tips + Tricks
> Consider what skills are already in your players' repertoires. Starting out with an existing but unmastered skill can help make players feel confident and increase faculty.
> If possible, identify a core skill that can act as the main method of interaction with the game. A simple but infinitely evolvable skill is a powerful thing, and worth searching for.

- With a list of possible skills in hand, rank them in terms of difficulty, complexity, and how natural they are for your players. This will help you narrow the field.
- Choose skills that have long learning curves and can be developed over longer time frames. Flipping a light switch at an expert level is fairly quickly achieved, while navigating by the stars is a lifelong pursuit.
- For longer/richer games, consider how skills can be broken down into smaller and more manageable subskills. Think about how to nest them, one inside the other, adding up to something complex.
- Consider: does this skill seem valuable to your players? If not, how could you make it valuable within the game?
- Are the skills you're considering measurable? How might you make them measurable? This often requires the use of new technology or active monitoring.

Step Five: Choose the Resistance

Good games are inherently uncertain. As a behavioral game designer, you get to determine what kind of uncertainty your players will have to overcome. Remember, resistance is a balancing act. You're trying to create an experience that keeps players in a state of flow, where their skills and the challenges they face are matched—stretching them just enough to develop those skills and learn something new. Too much resistance, and the game is frustrating and disheartening. Too little, and it's boring. Because resistance is an overarching part of the experience, it often interacts with other building blocks to serve its purpose. For example, a game may use scarcity (a form of resistance) to limit the resources available to players. Because of this, designing the resistance in a behavioral game is one of the most difficult and sophisticated parts of the process. The tension that a behavioral game creates, and the relief that comes from conquering that resistance, is the delicate dance you must orchestrate.

In the case of our student, we need to choose resistance carefully, as there is already a lot of resistance in the activity itself. As you'll recall from the player profile, our player isn't inclined to study, so her desire to avoid studying altogether is working against the objectives of our behavioral game. To offset this, we need to create some clever resistance that will change this dynamic. Scarcity is a form of resistance that can help us out here. Because our student is motivated by control, we'll introduce a scarce resource that she'll have to manage (which should increase her sense of autonomy). Additionally, we'll use some measure of time as another form of resistance, since duration plays a role in studying.

Tips + Tricks

> Be creative. Imagine as many forms of resistance as you can and then determine which ones would lead to the best gameplay. Scarcity, chance, and puzzles are just a few popular forms of resistance.

> Simple forms of resistance can create incredibly complex games. Don't try to make things too clever.

> Forced decisions that involve tradeoffs or comparisons can be a very effective form of resistance (if you do x, you lose y).

> In the same way we looked for skills that were expandable and long-term, consider forms of resistance that have equally long lives. If resistance can be grokked and overcome too quickly, it won't provide much uncertainty or engagement.

Step Six: Choose the Resources

Every game requires certain supplies in order to be played, and other optional resources can make things even more interesting. The options for action available to players increase in proportion to the resources available to them. Playing soccer with *three* balls would radically alter the choices available to the players. To choose the resources for your behavioral game, think about the basic supplies required for the activity you've chosen. Are they all necessary to build the skills you selected? Are there any you can take away? Build a basic supplies list. Next, think about what could help your players along in their quest. What would introduce new dynamics into the game? What would appeal to their player profile?

In the case of our student, a space to study, schoolbooks, and the Internet are obvious resources. Depending upon our student's habits, we may want to eliminate the Internet to aid focus. Recalling from the last step that we chose to create some scarcity and let our player manage a resource, let's introduce a made-up currency (inherently a scarce resource) into our game. We'll give our player tokens that she can use to buy exactly what she wants most: time *not* studying.

Tips + Tricks

> Don't take anything for granted. Consider every possible resource that is involved in the activity. Examine the impact of each on the overall experience.

> Consider which existing resources are helping or hindering your players' progress. Make adjustments accordingly.

> When inventing new resources to add into the mix, think about how they'll involve and interact with your other building blocks.

> Remember, not every behavioral game needs new resources. Sometimes the basics are enough. Start *limiting* resources (and letting players earn them back) before you jump to add more.

Step Seven: Define the Skill Cycle(s)

For players to learn or improve a skill in a behavioral game, that skill needs to be put into practice. Skill cycles are the way we accomplish this—an articulation of what it means to *actually play the game*. A skill cycle is much like a "round" in a normal game, and it's made up of all the central building blocks in the Game Frame: actions, black box, feedback, skills, resources, and resistance.

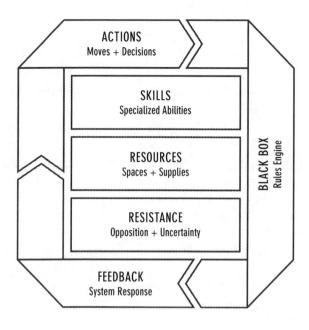

A skill cycle is one "period" during which actions are taken and feedback is delivered. Depending on the nature of the activity, this period could last one minute or one month. Ideally, a skill cycle should adopt the interval that best demonstrates the skill put to good use. In specifying a skill cycle, you are essentially explaining the "rules of play" to your players, which is why this step is most heavily related to the black box. The skill cycle is the general outline of how the game is played, what options for action are available to them, and what feedback they'll receive. The feedback that is provided must be tailored to the challenge at hand. A chef preparing a meal likely doesn't need feedback on average knife speed, but could definitely use a temperature readout on the stove. In a behavioral game where a desired action is arriving at work on time, the designer will have to account for how to respond to someone being late. In order to make sure a behavioral game achieves its purpose, defining a skill cycle for *every chosen skill* in the game is recommended.

In the case of our student, we have two skills in play; time management and focus, so we'll need two skill cycles running in tandem to create a holistic experience.

To create the skill cycle for *time management*, we'll begin by defining some time-based variables. The skill cycle will be one week in duration. Study hours will begin at 5:00 p.m. and end at 10:00 p.m. every weeknight. Our student must complete ten hours of study each week to continue playing. Every Monday, our student will receive fifteen tokens good for one hour of free time *during* study hours. Beginning at 5:00 p.m. each day, our referee (a parent) will ask our player if she plans to study or pay out a token for an hour of freedom. The student then has a decision to make. She faces that decision every hour until she elects to study, or until study hours end for the night. Once the student has completed two hours of study on any given night, no further tokens will be required for that evening's remaining free time. Meaning, if the student studies for two hours every day starting at 5:00 p.m., she will have fifteen tokens left at the end of the week. Alternatively, if the student trades in five tokens every night, she will run out by the end of the third day, and will be forced to study for five hours two nights in a row.

To create the skill cycle for *focus*, we'll reduce the duration of the study hours to thirty minutes initially, and add fifteen minutes to the total each week, eventually working our way up to the necessary two hours of study per night. This would require that we also adjust the weekly allotment of tokens accordingly. This also presupposes that we define the characteristics of "focus time" with our student, so that she understands our expectations. To add some visual feedback to the mix, we might place a large countdown clock (or timer) in our student's study area. And as an incentive to hunker down, we will award a bonus token to our student on any night where she exceeds the required study time by one hour or more.

Tips + Tricks

- Consider what skills are being mastered through the course of your game, and how to combine them with new ones to keep things fresh.
- Make sure the actions available to your players directly affect their progress in the game.
- Remember, a wider variety of available actions will make players feel more autonomous, but can also complicate things quickly.
- Options for action should be abundantly clear. Make sure your players know the moves available to them (unless you're purposefully trying to get them to explore their options as a form of resistance).
- Make sure that your skill cycles have an obvious beginning and end, whether that be time-based (daily, weekly, monthly) or action-based (every ten swings).
- Think about your skill cycle. Does it provide a steady stream of escalating challenge? What could change between cycles to ensure that?
- Watch for skills that are getting burned out or are no longer satisfying to use, and remember to increase resistance or combine them with newer skills to keep players engaged.
- The more specific the actions in your skill cycle are, the more specific your feedback should be.
- Know your black box and the rules governed by it. You should have a specific form of feedback in mind for every possible action (including inaction).

Step Eight: Choose the Outcomes

Every game has outcomes that occur en route to victory. The ultimate objective may take weeks, months, or even years to achieve, but along the way, players need to see and feel incremental successes and failures. Outcomes allow this. In terms of design, outcomes are related to short-term goals. If a short-term goal is accomplished or an opportunity missed, an outcome can drive the learning home. In many cases, outcomes take the form of rewards (tangible or intangible), but outcomes can actually be positive or negative. Our players may experience setbacks in their quest; sometimes they'll have to press reset and start over. If all the outcomes in a behavioral game are positive, uncertainty goes down (and takes learning with it).

In the case of our student, the skill cycle for focus offers the outcome of bonus tokens when our student studies longer than the required time. For the time management skill cycle, we'll need a juicier outcome, simply because the activity itself (studying) is not terribly entertaining, at least in its present state. So, every token that our student has left over at the end of the week can be traded in for some kind of prize. If possible, we'll try to make these prizes constructive, such as a new book or video game of her choice. And one more twist (which we'll keep secret): the prize for having ten tokens left over is more than than twice as good as the prize for five. Meaning, each additional token saved is worth more than the last. That should intrigue our player when first discovered, and it's likely that she'll then try to save all fifteen tokens to see what happens.

Tips + Tricks

> Remember that outcomes can be contingent or scheduled. Players can trigger an outcome based on a specific action they take, or a time frame within the game.
> Outcomes can occur based on ratios (a number of specific actions) and intervals (a unit of time) between outcomes.
> Remember what you learned from operant conditioning about rewards schedules: if they are variable/unpredictable you'll get a more active response as players try to grok the system.

Step Nine: Play-Test and Polish

With the pieces of your behavioral game now in place, it's time to put it through the paces. What's working about it? What isn't?

What are the risks if it backfires? What's going to keep it interesting in ten weeks' time? What have you not considered? Remember, your goal here is an elegant and engaging structured learning experience. When done right, radically simple or embedded behavioral games may be so natural and fluid that your players don't even know they're playing. They may simply assume that *this is the way things work*, or be sucked in by a particularly engaging skill cycle, and never question why. The military, which benefits from many game mechanics, is a perfect example of this.

In the case of our study game, we'll want to consider how it evolves over time. The time management aspect could become a mastered skill within a couple months, and then our student will be looking for something new to capture her attention.

Tips + Tricks

> Lower the barriers to entry—make it as easy as possible to play. The more a game asks of players in the beginning, the less likely they are to engage.

> Ensure that novelty has been built into the process across the board. A good behavioral game should be full of surprises and new things to grok.

> Add and subtract from your building blocks to see what happens to the experience. In our studying example, would adding time pressure (or social pressure) make it more engaging, or too frantic and stressful?

> Make sure the overall game experience is not *too* hard. Players thrive on repeated success, and the progress that it implies.

> Consider the role of technology in your behavioral game. How would the experience differ if you used more or less technology to enable feedback?

> Is the game personal enough for your players? Do they feel that it's tailored to their own unique personality and desires?

> Remember, above all, your work as a designer is never done. Keep raising the stakes. When your players reach their objectives, it's time to go back to the drawing board!

GAME FRAME

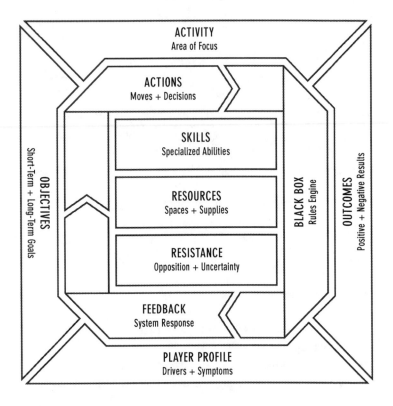

The Search Begins

At this point you've familiarized yourself with a framework and a process for designing behavioral games. But this is just the beginning. As a behavioral game designer, your job is to search for new and better ways to apply the ideas outlined here. The real power of bringing game dynamics to everyday life has yet to be realized, as we're only now beginning to understand the strange intersection between play and purpose. With this in mind, we can view the world through the Game Frame, and find inspiration in unlikely places.

The building blocks of behavioral games come in many shapes and sizes. One game's form of resistance is chance, while another's is competition. Over the course of my research, I've come across a handful of these variations that caught my eye for their simplicity and power. This level profiles those elements—popular forms of specific building blocks that will inspire and inform the design process. Included in each profile is a brief description of the concept, examples from the real world, and a few basic instructions for applying it to your designs.

In assembling these profiles I was surprised to find that certain building blocks, namely resistance, feedback, and resources, benefit from more variety of form than all the others combined. Some, such as activity, player profile, skills, and the black box, have been omitted entirely, as they are typically too bespoke to be useful as thought-starters.

I suspect that the building blocks with the most variety continue to expand because they offer designers enormous creative freedom. They are not limited by the number of skills we have, or the actions we can take. They are limited only by our imagination. Which means that this is not now, nor will it ever be, a comprehensive list. In the coming weeks and months, you'll likely find dozens of new variations on these building blocks and the dynamics they create. It is my sincere hope that as you do, you'll share them on the Game Frame website to benefit the rest of us. I'll do the same.

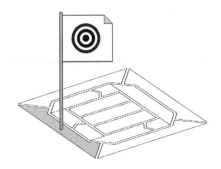

TARGETS

In Other Words: Benchmark, Bull's-eye, Quota

A target is a fixed goal, something specific we can aim for. Targets are typically spatial, as in a bull's-eye or basketball hoop, but can also be quantifiable, as in a revenue goal or speed record. As a form of the objectives building block, targets can be either short-term or long-term in nature. In general, they tend to be more concrete than other goals. Skill cycles are often structured around short-term goals designed to be achieved within that time frame. We should focus on those targets that can fit into our skill cycles most readily.

A lack of targets leads to aimless activity and confusion about degrees of success. When games don't offer us a clear idea of what precise performance looks like, we play with less purpose.

Case: Kickstarter.com

Everyone has a dream project waiting in the wings. Some people want to write a movie, others want to open a vegan bakery. Realizing these visions back in reality is anything but easy. To do that, you need money, time, and support. You'd have to rally your boss, your parents, your friends, and people you don't even know yet. What's more, they don't even know what you're dreaming about. That's where Kickstarter comes in. Kickstarter is an online funding platform for artists, designers, filmmakers, musicians, journalists, inventors, explorers, and everyone else with an idea. What the site does brilliantly is turn your project into a fund-raising target, making your goal *everyone's* goal. Every project on the site has a specific funding goal and a time limit. Visitors to your project pledge to support it with hard-earned cash, but with a twist: if your project doesn't hit its target for funding, then everyone gets their money back and nothing is produced. If you *do* get fully funded, the money is released to you, and your donors receive whatever products, prizes, and involvement you promised them. Needless to say, a disproportionate number of Kickstarter projects get funded, because a target for donations is far more concrete than any other kind of support we might give to our fellow dreamers.

Other Cases

> Reported to have begun in Amsterdam, urinal flies—small decals of house flies stuck to the insides of urinals, trigger the targeting instinct in men, reducing spillage/splash by up to 80 percent.

> Many athletes train by focusing on a target heart rate, a range that enables their heart and lungs to have a beneficial workout.

> Sales teams all over the world create monthly, quarterly, and annual quotas that specify the target sales volume expected of each salesperson.

> 4chan.org, a rogue message board community, set specific vote targets for the nominees of *Time* magazine's World's Most Interesting Person title—targets selected to make the first initials of the names on the list spell out "marblecake"—with 4chan's leader "moot" at the top of the list.

Why Targets Work

Targets seem to activate a primal desire within us—to hunt and pursue something we desire. The presence of anything that *stands out* is enough to trigger that impulse. Concentration and commitment to an objective are quite beneficial traits for a hunter/gatherer. Until recently, humans had to find (and in some cases subdue) the food we ate. That required a specialized focus that is not unique to us. Many species (including house cats) prowl, stalk, scavenge, and hunt. In the modern world, that pursuit can be focused on more abstract prey. A sales target isn't a buffalo, but it does put food on the table.

Instructions for Designing with Targets

Designing a behavioral game with targets is no different from working with any other objective. But with targets, you should be thinking about how that objective is presented. Is it visual? Is it quantifiable? Does it stand out? In fundraising, organizations don't just mention their sponsorship goal, they put a thermometer on the wall and watch it fill up. People going out to meet someone special don't wear nondescript clothing, they try to stand out and *become* a target. Think about the objectives in your game, then try to make them more specific, more in your face, and more taunting. Your players will fixate on them.

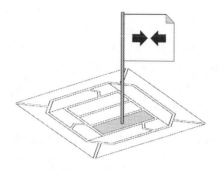

COMPETITION

In Other Words: Rivalry, Opponent, Adversary

Competition is a manifestation of the natural rivalry created when people and organizations clash over common desires. Competition is a dynamic that often produces a distinct feeling of motivation and aggression. The vast majority of the sports world is built on it. Competition also shows up in the workplace, where employees struggle to climb the corporate ladder, often at the expense of their peers. While many emotions are uniformly characterized as positive or negative, competitiveness is unique in that it can be viewed as constructive or destructive depending on the attitude and sportsmanship behind it.

A lack of competition can lead to confusion about what it means to win, and a loss of intensity in the activity itself. The presence of competition is often necessary to create and maintain a benchmark of success or quality.

Case: Passlogix

In a recent blog post, management consultant Peter Bregman relayed a story that wonderfully captures the power of competition in everyday life. Several years ago, his client Passlogix was experiencing an issue with their software—it wasn't working with an older version of Sun Microsystems, and that was a problem.

Passlogix CTO Marc Manza tried to solve the problem directly, but Sun wasn't particularly interested in solving compatibility issues with outdated software. So, the Passlogix team was tasked with finding a solution. They tackled it like any other problem. Two years later, with tons of sunk costs and no clear progress or solution, Marc tried something totally different. He bought a Nintendo Wii, brought it into the office, and announced a competition. The first person to solve the software problem—in their spare time—would be awarded the Wii. The problem was completely solved in two weeks. Viewing the problem as their job, the engineers at Passlogix couldn't solve it, but by introducing a little healthy competition, Marc was able to completely turn the situation on its head.

Other Cases

> Nike's new interactive street game, Nike Grid, pitted runners against each other on the streets of London, using only pay phones and the spirit of competition to drive involvement.

> Reality shows like *Top Chef* or *The Apprentice* thrive on competition, pitting people against each other to bring out the best (and worst).

> A recent study showed male skateboarders landed more tricks successfully (and aborted tricks less often) when a female rated as "highly attractive" was present.

> Competition transforms even the simplest activity—spelling— into a watchable televised event (the Scripps National Spelling Bee).

Why Competition Works

Having evolved in an environment that promotes survival of the fittest, we have a unique sensitivity to competition; any chance to prove ourselves as skilled and worthy should be taken. In the early days of our existence, human beings without the will to win didn't last long. Today, our competitive instinct is like any other natural impulse: given the right trigger, we start it up. Rivalry is such a strong cultural force that it can transcend generations in sports and, unfortunately, war.

Instructions for Designing with Competition

Ensure that your competition is structured fairly, and that the rules of engagement are clear and understood by everyone. Lack of clarity in highly competitive environments can lead to unpredictable behavior and a lack of trust in the system. Remember that competition manifests differently in different people. While some players are obvious in their will to win, others may satisfy that desire with more subtle means. Consider what kind of competition makes the most sense for your game and players.

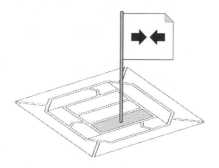

CHANCE

In Other Words: Randomness, Fortune, Luck

Chance is one of the oldest and most powerful forms of resistance. Since the early days of our species, humans have looked up to the heavens and wondered why things unfold the way they do. Why does fortune favor some and not others? So many of our cultural traditions, from rain dances to lucky numbers, exist as our attempt to influence fate. Chance can be implemented simply by introducing randomness and probability into a system.

A lack of chance can lead to predictability and boredom. The mere possibility of a random occurrence raises our alertness.

Once we know that chance isn't playing a role, we settle into the routine that best serves our purposes.

Case: Momofuku Ko

For several years now, a table at Momofuku Ko has been one of the toughest to get in New York City, and yet it doesn't give its scant thirty-two reservations per night away to celebs and big shots. It's packed because they'll give them to *anyone.* At 10:00 a.m. every day the restaurant website releases reservations for that same day the following week, on a first-come, first-served basis. Because so many people hit the site at that time, the reservations can be snatched up in two to three seconds, making success in the process largely a product of probability and perseverance. Unlike gambling, where you risk real money to win, Momofuku asks only that you risk a few minutes, and the upside is great—a delicious dinner that even the friends of the owner can't get without some good luck. The amazing food makes the reservations desirable, but the mechanics of chance makes them seem magical.

Other Cases

> ChatRoulette.com burst onto the scene last year by connecting random (and occasionally nude) strangers by video chat at the click of a button.
> Finance professor Peter Tufano developed a savings program in Michigan that targets individuals who typically don't save money by offering a monthly savings raffle as a bonus for depositing money.
> An iPhone game called Button asks users to simply press a graphic button whenever it lights up, awarding points and prizes randomly.
> To this day, we still resolve conflicts by flipping a coin, and we choose heads or tails as if it matters.

Why Chance Works

Our learning circuitry doesn't discriminate between experiences, so we view systems governed by randomness with the same scrutiny we apply to *any* novelty. After the surprise of winning money on a spin at the roulette table, our brain's pleasure centers light up, desperately seeking to explain why that happened, and how we can make it happen again. So, we lay out more money. We obsess over the game. We study it for patterns. We see ten black numbers in a row and think *it's got to be red this time*. Blaise Pascal and Pierre de Fermat started corresponding about the theory of probability in 1654. Over 350 years have passed, and you can still find people crowded around games of chance trying to figure out "a system." Although everyone is somewhat captivated by chance, there is variance in what kind of risks we're willing to take. Recent studies with rats suggest that deficiencies in neurotransmitters like serotonin and dopamine can lead humans to be more susceptible to gambling addiction.

Instructions for Designing with Chance

When designing a behavioral game that needs moments of excitement, consider using chance as a spice, peppered across the experience to keep things interesting. While on a diet, you might pack five brown bag lunches for the week and drop a candy bar in two of them. Consider that chance can also randomize repetitive experiences. Instead of the same staff meeting topics every week, you could have a bowl filled with the options that you draw from at random. In general, it's a good idea to pair chance with mechanics that focus on the development of skills, since chance never will.

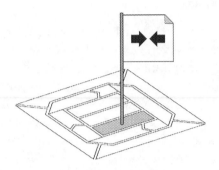

TIME PRESSURE

In Other Words: Urgency, Countdown, Timer

Time is fundamental to the human experience—it is the unit by which we measure the constant change of the world around us. But time is also elastic. We're not always aware of it, and in fact, as we have seen, certain activities can make it seem longer or shorter. Clocks, too, if we use them correctly, can make activities seem longer or shorter, and more or less intense. Time can easily be used as a resource or a form of feedback within a game, but it most often represents a form of resistance. It can be used to determine when the game takes place, and how long it (or a part of it) will last. This in turn has a huge impact on how we approach activities within the game. With limitless time to play, we lean back and explore. With time running out, we jump in and take brash action. Some games allow time to pass even as players are away, creating a sense of urgency to return to the system and tend to one's affairs.

A lack of time pressure in a game creates a casual pace, and asks players to regulate their own momentum. This can result in rich relaxed play, or a sense of aimlessness.

Case: Gilt Groupe

Sample sales are a tradition among high-end fashion brands, but one that most people can't enjoy, since they are often invitation-only and occur in fashion capitals like New York City and Paris. Gilt Groupe turned that notion on its head by developing a website that turns a sample sale into a bit of a behavioral game. Gilt .com remains invitation-only, and makes ample use of the prestige and scarcity inherent in luxury goods, but what makes the experience especially interesting is their use of time. Collections go on sale everyday at *12 o'clock sharp* Eastern time, and often sell out in less than an hour. In fact, over 100,000 visitors hit the site in the space of that one hour as they fight for their chance to snag last season's "it" items. This clever use of time pressure is certainly not the site's only key to success, but it does provide a wonderful sense of urgency, which is sometimes all you need.

Case: Target Checkout

One of the most important skills when you work a checkout counter is how fast you can move the line. During peak hours, a crush of customers can really back things up and the service experience can suffer as a result. Several years ago, Target began using a system to promote speed behind the register. The system tracks what items are being rung up, how long each item is *supposed* to take, and then rates cashiers on their performance per customer using a bold scoring system displayed right on the register's monitor. A "G" stands for green, which is acceptable speed, while an "R" stands for red which means too slow. The system also tracks the cashier's average performance over the course of dozens of sales, and calculates a percentage success rate. The speed score benchmark is 90 percent. Fall below that, and you could be in trouble. Exceed it, and you'll be up for raises and promotions. Clearly, Target is one place where having a quick draw really counts for something.

Other Cases

> Domino's Pizza famously turned delivery into a game by promising your pizza would arrive in thirty minutes or less (or it's free).
> Many advanced chess players play with a chess clock, allowing them to determine how much time they can spend considering moves, adding a layer of urgency to the game.
> Sporting events make masterful use of time, with game clocks governing everything from the overall length of the game to the shot clock that preserves basketball's fast-paced style of play.
> The hit television series *24* pioneered the use of real-time throughout its episodes, including commercials, showing how time can be a creative influence.

Why Time Pressure Works

As any good procrastinator will tell you, time pressure is the easiest way to create urgency. There is some evidence to suggest that the same neurotransmitters that regulate seeking behavior also regulate our sense of time. Time flies when you're having fun, and fun is flow. When we focus intently, our perception of time can slow or speed up depending on the situation. When the system we're playing limits time, it's possible that we shift into focus mode more readily because of this association between time and seeking. While the science may not be clear-cut, we know that having more or less time affects behavior and perception, immediately and broadly.

Instructions for Designing with Time Pressure

Use time pressure whenever you need to create a sense of urgency or, in cases where time is already limited and you plan to open it up, a sense of exploration. Think about how to display time— as a clock, a countdown, a rating of average time (as in the case of Target), or another method altogether. Consider what you are asking players to do within their allotted time, and how that expectation maps to reality. With longer time frames, such as the eight-hour workday, consider how to break the time up and create multiple waves of engagement around specific activities.

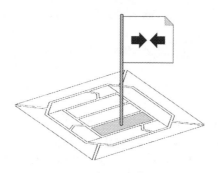

SCARCITY

In Other Words: Limited, Collectible, Rare

Scarcity is a lack of supply, a familiar concept to anyone who has studied modern economics. When the supply of a desired resource is low, demand goes up. The same is true in behavioral games. Anything quantifiable that players have to manage within a game could be made scarce. In some cases that could mean weapons and ammunition; in others, it might mean water or food supplies. Features and functionality of equipment and software count too. Some resources can be initially unavailable and be unlocked or obtained through exploration and experience. Scarcity in a game demands that players make careful choices about which resources they'll use, retain, pursue, collect, or ignore.

A lack of scarcity can lead to an experience that is too easy. A sailboat equipped with plentiful features like automatic navigation and sails is not going to demand your full attention. In terms of flow, this virtually ensures boredom.

Case: Meeting Tokens

Ask anyone working in corporate America today and they'll tell you: there are too many meetings. Mike Monteiro of Mule Design felt the same way, but he decided to do something about it. Mike designed and produced meeting tokens (good for fifteen minutes each) and asked all his project managers to use the tokens to pay each employee for their time in meetings. They would be given a certain number of tokens each week, and once they were gone, that was it. He also created and distributed to everyone a special red token called the Red Merlin (a tip of the hat to the creator of 43Folders.com, Merlin Mann). The Red Merlin ends any meeting on the spot. It's up to each individual to decide if and when his or her time is being wasted, and use the Red Merlin accordingly. While Mike didn't publicize the results of his experiment, the tokens were so popular on the web that full sets of them were eventually sold right from the Mule Feed Store. While these tokens might appear at first glance to be a kind of currency, it's important to note that they can't be earned. Everyone gets an allotted amount at the beginning of the week. This makes them scarce, and a resource to be managed.

Other Cases

> Some bakeries are known for selling their goods until they run out, then promptly closing up shop—customers show up earlier and earlier each day.
> Prestigious colleges like Stanford have a very limited number of available freshman openings, creating a near insane level of competition among overachieving high school seniors.
> Pokémon and other collectibles often come with a reminder to "collect them all"—a directive we find hard to resist.
> The "must have" toy every holiday season inevitably sells out, and the lack of availability leads to irrational behavior among parents, including ludicrous spending on eBay and other aftermarkets.

Why Scarcity Works

Scarcity is often associated with things of real value—food, shelter, mates, and other natural resources that are not available abundantly. As a result, when anything is scarce, our first instinct is to assume it has some kind of value. That's why we often see irrational behavior in the midst of scarcity. We also attempt to reduce scarcity by collecting. As hunter gatherers, we innately understand the value of building up a collection. Collecting and managing resources has many survival benefits, and we're naturals at both. Additionally, by forcing us to make choices about limited resources, behavioral games make those decisions meaningful.

Instructions for Designing with Scarcity

Scarcity is good for adding an element of competition in a multiplayer system, or adding an element of strategy and control in a single player system. Think about what your players need to accomplish their goals. Think about how you can take away resources and make them available through gameplay. Consider that scarcity is an invitation to explore, assuming that additional resources are out there. Remember that something as simple taking turns is a kind of scarcity. Each player has one chance to act in each round of play and must make the most of it. Anything that is necessary or helpful that can be limited can be made scarce. Now you must decide if and how players will get access to those resources. In many games, additional resources are offered at the end of a level or round of play, turning scarce items into rewards.

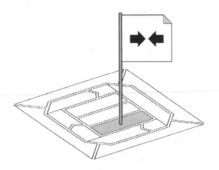

PUZZLES

In Other Words: Mysteries, Patterns, Hints

Puzzles are problems that promise the existence of a solution. In some ways, they satiate our desire to repeat the kind of perplexing experiences we encounter in real life. From birth, we are puzzled by countless interactions. How do I walk? How do I open the door? And one of the grandest puzzles of all: what is everyone saying and how do I communicate with them? The problem-solving skills that come from all this bewilderment serve us for the rest of our lives. Of course, puzzles come in too many forms to name—patterns, mazes, word games, plot twists—their common element being the existence of a solution, realization, prediction, or understanding. Because puzzles promise a solution while real world challenges offer us no such favor, we relish the chance to attack them.

A lack of puzzles reduces the chance for structured discovery, which can negatively impact volition. Why continue when no new realizations await? Also, the absence of puzzles can reduce engagement. It's too easy to get distracted when there's nothing to solve for. In the broadest sense then, a puzzle-free system or experience is a kind of shallow entertainment, and not really a game at all.

Case: Google Recruiting

In 2004, a strange billboard appeared on Highway 101 in Silicon Valley. Written in a plain black font, the billboard's message read, "{first 10-digit prime found in consecutive digits e}.com." Commuters passing by the billboard had no idea what to make of it. Who was behind it? And what was the point? For those brilliant minds that solved the puzzle, 7427466391.com led to a website with an another equation designed to test their skills further. Upon completing that, the visitor was directed to a Google Labs webpage that said, "One thing we learned while building Google is that it's easier to find what you're looking for if it comes looking for you. What we're looking for are the best engineers in the world. And here you are." Instead of approaching HR the same way as everyone else, Google took a chance, developed a game for recruiting, and let things play out. In addition to creating a ton of good PR, and showing Google's prospective employees that it had high standards, the game generated a flood of great candidates for the search giant.

Other Cases

> Oulipo is a rare club founded in 1960 by writers and mathematicians who sought to create written works using bizarre constraints such as a lipogram (writing that excludes one or more letters).

> Website BookOven.com lets a community of users copyedit new books one random line at a time—turning each line into a puzzle to be solved.

> Scavenger hunts and geocaching use hidden items and the subsequent search for them as a large-scale, location-based puzzle.

> Mystery novels, one of the most popular genres of books, are essentially one big puzzle, with clues and hints to solve the case shared along the way.

Why Puzzles Work

Puzzles are driven by the same cognitive processes we've already examined. The exhilaration of grokking a difficult puzzle, cracking a code, or finding an Easter egg lights up the reward circuitry in our brains. The fact that puzzles and other similarly designed experiences have a guaranteed solution drives even deeper engagement, since we needn't worry about the futility of the activity. There is an answer; we need only to find it.

Instructions for Designing with Puzzles

Most of the activities and skills that make up behavioral games have puzzles built right in. Learning to make a dress, for example, is a kind of puzzle. How you cut a pattern, and connect the pieces of that garment takes some figuring out. When designing a behavioral game, you can begin by improving the existing puzzles inherent in the activity. How can you make them clearer, more engaging, and more fun? Beyond that, you can use puzzles as a way to unlock new and different experiences within your game. Limited information can be a kind of puzzle. When players don't have all the information they need to make a decision or take action, they have to fill in the pieces. Puzzles are a test bed for creating the flow dynamic between challenge and skills. Attempting to solve a puzzle for which you do not have the skills or tools can lead to rapid demotivation. Always pair a challenge with your players' abilities to create the perfect amount of tension.

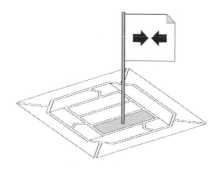

NOVELTY

In Other Words: Surprises, Changes, Curiosities

Novelty, the presence of anything new, is something our brains crave. As a form of resistance, novelty can have positive or negative effects, depending on the attitude of the players and the nature of what is being introduced. In general, people like to stick to a routine. We get stuck in our ways (and worldview) because we are "cognitive misers" and expending extra energy making sense of needless change is disadvantageous. But that dynamic can be turned on its head when change is something we have to process to achieve our goals. Then, the novelty is fascinating. Our bodies respond well to change too—interval training has shown that we respond more positively to different patterns of exercise than repetitive workouts. Novelty comes in many forms, including changes of scenery, patterns, processes, activities, and resources.

A lack of novelty leads to boredom. Change presents a new set of challenges and patterns, which in turn leads to flow and a sense of purpose. We're not always prepared for it, but we achieve an optimal state of mind when dealing with it.

Case: Seating Charts

In my company's New York office, we sit together in an open floor plan to conserve space and encourage collaboration. Islands built of eight desks host a mix of different roles and responsibilities, with little concern for seniority. Instead, we're very interested in what skills and abilities can be shared purely by proximity. While having a mixed and open seating plan is great, we don't stop there. Instead, a simple application of novelty is what really makes the office hum. Every three or four months, particularly when a new group of employees starts, we'll mix up the seating chart to force a reset of the office chemistry and social order. The first couple days of a new seating arrangement are disorienting—people are grokking a new pattern in the office. But within a week, the new connections being formed between employees are unmistakable. The office is like a buffet of unique personalities and talents—we're just using a little novelty to make sure everyone gets a taste.

Other Cases

> Sites like Facebook and Twitter have a secret weapon that other forms of media simply don't have—their content changes constantly and features people we care about, creating an unrivaled stream of personalized novelty.

> Apple is very proactive in using novelty to drive sales of their technology, announcing new and updated products on a regular schedule that creates unmatched anticipation.

> Trader Joe's stocks an ever-changing collection of unique products—creating a shopping treasure hunt—and sales per square foot are double that of other supermarkets.

> Retailers change their window displays regularly, to signal the promise of a new experience inside.

Why Novelty Works

We're surprised and perplexed when something doesn't match with our current worldview or our understanding of a system. That feeling represents an opportunity to learn something new and potentially beneficial about our environment. Therefore, our brains prioritize and reward novelty when we encounter it. It makes perfect sense, then, that routine change deployed within a system creates habitual behavior. Recent analysis of our addiction to email and web surfing has shown that these systems offer us a constant stream of new information and content, something our brains mistake as continually important (it may or may not be). These digital nuggets are triggering our seeking instinct.

Instructions for Designing with Novelty

To use novelty within a behavioral game, think about the day-to-day experience you're developing. What about it is stale? What about it is static but needn't be? Use novelty sparingly to challenge the assumptions of your players, give them new options, tools, and resources, and keep the experience fresh. Remember that today's digital culture has acclimated us to a pace of change that is hard to satisfy. To create a truly engaging experience, you'll be fighting for attention with all of the content the Internet has to offer. Consider letting your players dictate the pace of change by interacting with the system. Can you allow them to indicate when they want more novelty? Finally, remember that amidst *too much* change, players may become uncomfortable and search for something to ground themselves. Experiment with the right amount of change for your players.

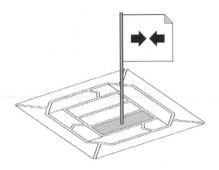

LEVELS

In Other Words: Stages, Areas, Domains

Levels are hierarchical and bounded domains in which we play. They also signify ability and access, because they are graduated and require qualifications to move among them. As individuals level up in a system, they get to enjoy a new set of challenges, abilities, and areas to explore. A twelfth grader has access to twelfth grade classes, activities, and privileges, while younger students do not. From a behavioral games perspective, we view levels as discrete challenges designed to move someone from a low degree of skill to a high one. Levels make an experience manageable, and isolate growth opportunities so that players can tackle challenges one at a time. If a new graduate was immediately given the full responsibilities of the CEO, she would surely experience anxiety and a sense of diminished faculty (a phenomenon we do see at some startups). By dividing the acquisition of those skills into several levels, the system of a business becomes more manageable.

A lack of levels can make acquiring skills a chaotic process, and confuse players about the direction they're supposed to be heading. Even a pause in the activity—some division between levels—allows players a chance to assimilate what they've learned.

Case: Come Sail Away

I recently discovered that I enjoy sailing, which was surprising, given that I grew up without a body of water in sight. Naturally, my first instinct was to set sail for the tropics, but I didn't know how to set a sail at all. So, I enrolled in a multiday sailing course in New York that was designed to teach me the basics. It wasn't long before I began to realize that sailing had designated experience levels. And these levels exist out of necessity. Sailing is an activity that ranges wildly in difficulty and complexity, from the simple act of "tacking" on a lake in calm wind, to navigating in massive swells and inclement weather in the middle of the Atlantic ocean. Any learning curve *that* steep needs to be divided into manageable chunks. Here are just a few of the courses (each one filled with dozens of skills) that go into becoming a competent sailor: Basic Keelboat, Basic Cruising, Bareboat Cruising, Coastal Navigation, Coastal Passage Making, Celestial Navigation, Offshore Passage Making. And that doesn't include the various levels of crew or instructor certification that exist, all based on how many hours you've been out on the boat. With basic keelboat certification under my belt, I am moving up the path to legitimacy, and the levels make it seem achievable.

Other Cases

> Ski resorts rank skiers into beginner, intermediate, and expert classes, and then assign levels to the runs on the mountain—green circle, blue square, and black diamond.
> Global jet-setters on Dopplr.com often see each new city as a level to be grokked, competing on how many cities they've visited, and their knowledge of local hotspots.
> In many martial arts, different belt levels (brown, red, black) offer new sets of skills and challenges, from breaking boards to working with weapons.
> Many popular sports have a complex hierarchy, with multiple classifications in high school, college, and professional play.

Why Levels Work

Levels work by focusing our attention on a defined area of exploration. Moving beyond or beating a level requires specific knowledge and skills. The promise of a *next* level where any number of novelties await us, along with any rewards we might receive for leveling up, is enough to trigger our desire. The feeling of using skills that we already have, coupled with the development of new ones, is infectious. Levels also help with issues of *faculty*, by providing a clear roadmap for progress. Don't worry about anything else, *just focus on beating level one.*

Instructions for Designing with Levels

To use levels effectively, think about the skills that need to be developed over the course of your behavioral game. What do players need to be able to do at the highest level? Now examine how you might break up the challenges that are part of improving these skills. If you can create tiers of meaningful and clear challenge, and control access to these tiers, you'll have a good level system in place. In golf lessons for example, it's not uncommon to start beginners off with just a seven-iron and a putter. Once comfortable with these basics, players can level up and add clubs to their bag to take on the additional complexity and challenge of selecting and hitting with different clubs. Keep in mind though, that some experiences require a broader palette of choices to be fun (painting with *one* color is not very exciting), so make sure that your first level is interesting from the outset.

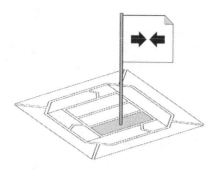

SOCIAL PRESSURE

In Other Words: Peer Pressure, Obligation, Conformity

Social pressure is a form of influence exerted by the people around us. Our desire to belong is one of the strongest human emotions, and so we're often acutely aware of what is expected of us. To be a part of the group means members must meet some basic criteria and accepted norms. These criteria may evolve or change based on the needs of the group or the world at large. Manifestations of these norms vary widely. We also pay strict attention to the movements and patterns of the herd. What the majority of us do *must* be right. This idea is often referred to as "social proof." For example, it's totally normal to assume that a fully booked restaurant must be delicious.

A lack of social pressure leads to a lack of obligation or belonging. However, the world is full of people, and any hint of social scrutiny will alter behavior, whether it's a function of a game or not.

Case: The TED Conference

Every year, a couple thousand of the most powerful and influential people in the world meet in California for one week of mind-blowing presentations and demonstrations on ideas worth spreading. Known as the TED Conference, this event is able to get people who are notorious for being inaccessible and extremely busy to turn off their computers, clear their schedules, and spend five relaxing days in conversation with their peers. Everyone is mentally present. Everyone is respectful. Everyone approaches the week with humility and wonder. So why is it that these world-renowned CEOs, authors, professors, and celebrities are so well-behaved? Because everyone else is. The conference has been going on for decades now, and practices that were started long ago have become the social norm. No matter how crazy and exclusive their day-to-day existence is, when TED attendees check in, they leave their baggage at the door, and adopt the identity of the group.

Other Cases

> Private clubs for everything from golf to knitting dominate our culture, and their users define and enforce the standards and practices of membership.
> In an experiment by Matthew Salganik featuring an artificial music market, it was shown that simply showing the popularity of a song could influence how often it was downloaded and how listeners rated it.
> Social games like *Mafia Wars* work primarily because they prey on our social obligations and compulsions—success in these games is dependent on pressuring the people around you to play along.
> The Social Workout Challenge puts a community of people together to support each other in reaching fitness goals.

Why Social Pressure Works

Our survival is more likely if we operate in the company of others who are working to ensure our health and safety. Our brain has evolved to help us interact with and understand other people. You need only to ask a seventh grader why "fitting in" is important to understand how basic this drive is. Playing in the company of others triggers a type of self-awareness that has developed over thousands of years filled with social dynamics. In general, we're very concerned about what other people are doing, and how they're perceiving us. This is known as the Hawthorne effect, a theory that people adjust their behavior to conform to the expectations or norms of the people around them. For example, a recent GameSpy report showed that the more friends someone has in a game, the less likely they are to cheat.

Instructions for Designing with Social Pressure

You can use social pressure to promote certain behavior norms, encourage achievement, or create aspirational energy within a system. Think about the various ways you can bring social pressure to life—from group feedback to public activity. Anything that makes players feel like they are part of something or desire to be part of something is useful. Make sure that there is a clear group identity—some invisible threshold that keeps it together.

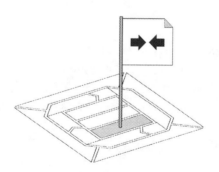

TEAMWORK

In Other Words: Collaboration, Cooperation, Co-Creation

Teamwork is the act of more than one player working together toward a common goal. Although typically promoted as a positive and helpful dynamic, teamwork can also act as a form of resistance, because other people represent a force outside our control. The benefits of collaboration are many, but before they can be realized, a team must learn how to work together. This process can be frustrating and challenging (as in a three-legged race) but also produce great results. Friction within teams happens routinely in sports, but also in business and online social platforms. In working together, we are subjected to the input, actions, and desires of other players, which influences our approach to the game. Our input, actions, and desires in turn influence them. Collaborative processes are often iterative and unstructured, allowing recombinant thinking and incongruent feedback to guide us to new heights. Recently, collaborative problem solving has been enabled online such that hundreds or thousands of participants can work together—giving rise to the notions of crowd intelligence.

A lack of collaboration and teamwork can lead to isolation, and a slower learning curve over the long term. Without the help of co-conspirators to guide our growth, we have to rely on the system alone to mold our thoughts and actions.

Case: Toastmasters

Public speaking is not easy, and most people are too embarrassed to get onstage frequently enough to get good at it. With this in mind, Toastmasters turned public speaking into a behavioral game by turning the audience into a team. Every meeting is a learn-by-doing workshop, where participants give speeches to each other and receive feedback on their performance. Importantly, there is no instructor in a Toastmasters meeting—only fellow players. Everyone is accountable for learning and promoting best practices, because everyone's improvement depends on everyone else.

Other Cases
> ➤ A new collaborative problem-solving platform from IDEO called OpenIDEO is pitting the minds of its players against the world's most difficult social challenges.

> Odyssey of the Mind is an educational program that asks teams of students to solve complex problems like: "Design, build, and run a vehicle that uses mousetraps as its only source of energy."

> Popular collaboration exercises using LEGO blocks demonstrate the challenge of team communication: in one version managers have to direct builders who aren't allowed to see what they're building.

> Quirky.com turns product development into a collaborative game, complete with cash awards for the people who help make the products come to life.

Why Teamwork Works

When we share common goals, we share success. But when we have to count on the performance of others, this creates tension. Before we can benefit from having a team, we have to build trust and fluid communication. Having a chance to explain our approach (and hear theirs), increases our sense of faculty. Once committed to a plan, knowing that other people are counting on us creates a strong sense of urgency and accountability.

Instructions for Designing with Teamwork

Using teamwork in a behavioral game requires that you have multiple players trying to accomplish the same objective, and that working together is required to succeed. Remember, teamwork is not just support, it's conflict. Consider how you can force players to confront their communication gap and find new ways to achieve their individual and collective objectives.

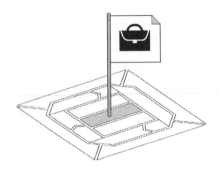

CURRENCY

In Other Words: Economy, Marketplace, Exchange

Currency is a medium of exchange. It's a way of standardizing value so that players can trade goods, services, and rights with each other, or the game itself. The concept of currency is quite familiar to us, since our real-world economy is itself built around it. This economy has taught us that currency is *representative* of value, but not static; it can become more or less valuable in different circumstances. No matter where we are (real or virtual), the basic economic principles of currency still apply. Anything that can be exchanged for something of value will be collected and attended to.

Without a common currency, conducting any kind of business can be difficult. Absent any clear mechanism for earning, buying, or trading what seem to be important resources in the game, many players will suffer a crisis of faculty, and disassociate entirely.

Case: The Arcade

One of the most powerful examples of currency in a behavioral game dates back to the early 1900s. At that time, bowling inspired the invention of an arcade game that would become synonymous with fun: skee ball. Skee ball is part of a family of "redemption games" in which currency takes the form of little red tickets. The better a player performs, the more tickets he receives. These tickets can then be traded for prizes at a central location in the arcade. These systems are economically brilliant because players put real money into the game, which *converts* that money into tickets (at a great exchange rate for the arcade), and thus abstracts the value equation. Suddenly a Chinese finger trap that could be obtained at a toy store for fifty cents becomes the result of ten dollars in gameplay. What's more, because we tend to justify our efforts after the fact, the prizes in the arcade are perceived as more valuable than they would be in any other setting.

Case: OMGPOP.com

The website OMGPOP.com is a social gaming platform, where people from all over the world come together to play casual games. But founder Charles Forman and the site's management team knew that encouraging visitors to stick around and engage with a site over the long term is challenging. So, they built a behavioral game on top of it. OMGPOP awards users with points for almost every action on the site, from logging in every day (the site cleverly awards more and more points for each consecutive day you come back), to playing and winning games with other people. This simple mechanism shows users which behaviors the system values, and gives a special significance to simple actions that are almost subconscious on other sites. Rather than stopping at points, though, OMGPOP uses them as a currency, allowing users to spend them to unlock experiences and objects on the site in a handful of virtual shops.

Other Cases

> Frequent flier miles, the original currency of loyalty, were so influential that they changed an entire industry.

> Game development company Seriosity has created a special add-on for Microsoft Outlook called *Attent*, which allows

users to attach a currency called Serios to their outgoing emails, signaling what's important and reducing inbox clutter.

> The famed McDonald's *Monopoly* sweepstakes offers game pieces attached to certain products—some of which are instant currency (good for free food), and others that are part of a set with far bigger prizes.

> Casinos use chips for convenience and security, but also because they create some abstraction from real money and thus increase spending.

Why Currency Works

Currency works out of necessity. In a culture of specialized trades—where one person raises cattle and another grows grain—a system of exchange becomes a requirement. One person may not need the assets of another, but everyone's assets need a market value for fair trade. A currency simplifies our desire to possess and experience many things; all things can be bought with money.

Instructions for Designing with Currency

Currency works best when you have levels or resources that players want to access. To use a currency, determine whether it will be physical or virtual, what the exchange rate will be, and how it will be used. Like any form of reinforcement, currency can be positive or negative (players can buy things they like, or pay to avoid things they don't). Keep in mind that showing the rate of exchange for a unit of currency can sometimes hurt you—when credit cards started blatantly showing the cash value of their loyalty points, those points lost some of their luster. Our rational side can always calculate their true value, but our inner player is happy to toil away without destroying this illusion. What's most important in deploying currency is ensuring that it is used in service of a larger goal or purpose, and not just to create a secondary economy.

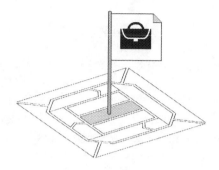

RENEWAL

In Other Words: Regeneration, Iteration, Boost

Renewal is a process of replenishment. One of the most wondrous and powerful things about games is that you can start over. You can try and fail, and try again. You can die and be reborn. You can risk it all, and still have fun. Games have all kinds of devices for allowing us to regenerate and renew. They have discoverable resources known as "power-ups," which replenish our hit points, life force, mana, or whatever the measure of our vitality might be. Action games sometimes feature auto-regenerative health, where simply surviving for a certain amount of time allows you to grow stronger. And innumerable games offer us some way to earn extra lives or chances to succeed. Games give us room to fail, and even if they limit us with some scarcity (three lives per game for instance), this room allows us to stretch and grow unencumbered.

A lack of renewal can make things too serious—even read. Most situations where we're not allowed mistakes have serious consequences. Unfortunately, if you fail in college, you're out. If you fail at work, you're fired. No do-overs. Which is unfortunate, because do-overs are exactly what we need to develop complex skills.

Case: Showering at Work

A bizarre eight-week productivity study in the United Kingdom asked the employees of a handful of companies to take a midday shower break to see if it impacted their overall productivity. The results were pretty astounding. Average productivity went up 42 percent, and creativity was boosted as well. The results are significant for many industries, because the study included a restaurant, architecture firm, lingerie manufacturer, and an advertising agency, all of which benefited from these showers. One possible explanation for the improvement is that the showers acted as an opportunity to reset and recharge; they were power ups! Participants discussing the experience were quoted using words like "pick me up" and "refuel"; sure signs that the showers represented not just a break, but a renewal of energy.

Other Cases

> In *Monopoly*, you get $200 every time you pass go, in *RISK*, a few new soldiers with every turn, and in Scrabble, new tiles after using your current set.

> A fun and physical manifestation of renewal is the Copenhagen Wheel, a bicycle wheel innovation created by MIT students that allows energy from braking to be released later as a boost of power.

> Each state has its own system of points for traffic offenses, essentially awarding more points for more severe infractions—a form of renewal follows, where simply by driving incident-free these points are slowly removed from your license.

> From our legal system's "three strikes" policy, to carnival games and sports, we're very interested in how many chances we get, and ways to earn more.

Why Renewal Works

Renewal is a basic principle of life. Healing, sleeping, and seasons are based on the notion that life can rebuild. What's interesting about the idea of renewal in games is that additional lives and chances to play are just about continuing the game experience. This is why they're not really rewards; they're resources that give us permission to continue. And yet, we strive for them. Sadly, in real world environments, you seldom see this kind of behavior. No one is trying to earn an extra work day, likely because they don't want to be there.

Instructions for Designing with Renewal

Consider the resources that are required in your system. Think about the ways that players can fail, or hit a dead end. Then create a way for your players to begin again. Remember that renewal does not have to be infinite. Even a second chance can help. Your system is balanced when the renewal encourages players without providing them undue advantage.

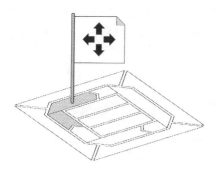

FORCED DECISIONS
In Other Words: Choice, Preference, Judgment

Forced decisions are choices that have to be made to continue an activity. Games do a great job at creating these moments. Unlike so many experiences in life where it's unclear what our options are, games communicate choices and options constantly. Perhaps a path or route must be chosen. Or we have to decide whether to stay and fight, or escape and battle another day. In these cases, we can quickly determine the available options, deliberate, and make our choice. If we don't, the action stops, or worse, we lose. In many board games and social games too, the concept of taking turns is a mechanic for forcing decisions. It's *your* turn, and it's time to make something happen.

A lack of decisions and choices can leave players feeling powerless. If they can't make choices, the activity may not be a game at all. Books and movies differ strongly from games in this regard: nothing you decide is going to change how the movie ends. A cliffhanger ending, where the story is finished in the imagination of the audience, is a popular exception to this rule.

Case: *Rangefinders*

One of my favorite examples of the power of decisions within a behavioral game comes from Byron Reeves and J. Leighton Read, authors of *Total Engagement*. They propose installing a kind of "surveillance game" at high-profile venues, such as Grand Central Station. Today, security teams likely watch multicamera screens for hours on end, passively looking for something suspicious. In the game described by Reeves and Read, entitled *Rangefinders*, an augmented reality program projects "good guys" and "bad guys" into Grand Central's video feed alongside the real commuters. These virtual people blend in and challenge the security team to identify signs of wrongdoing on a minute-by-minute basis. Because these virtual bad guys show up regularly, and the security team is penalized when they make it through the terminal undetected, team members are highly engaged—actively making decisions about each and every person that comes across their screen. Friend or foe? It sounds like science fiction, but it's probably not too far off.

Case: *Lucky* Magazine

Lucky magazine is a popular women's fashion magazine that focuses specifically on shopping. Near the front of the magazine, readers encounter a full page of stickers with the exclamations YES! and MAYBE? on them. The intent of these stickers is straightforward: as readers flip through the magazine, they mark the items they want, as well as those they might want to revisit later. Unbeknownst to the readers, these stickers are forcing decisions, which adds focus to the experience of reading the magazine. While most other magazines are enjoyed as a passive activity, *Lucky* challenges readers with something more involved.

Other Cases

> The extreme popularity of the NCAA Tournament is due in part to the custom brackets created by tens of millions of fans—each making predictions about the games to come.
> The now classic *Choose Your Own Adventure* books were among the most engaging young adult fiction ever released, and brought a new level of interactivity to the bookshelf.
> A popular YouTube video series entitled *How to Pick Up Girls* offered viewers a chance to choose what they would do, and the video series unfolded accordingly.
> CommandShift3.com forces you to choose the prettier of two websites over and over again, creating a database of preference and aesthetic rank.

Why Forced Decisions Work

Forced decisions have two benefits that align well with our psychological needs and tendencies. First, having a choice can increase feelings of control and intrinsic motivation, enhancing our sense of self. The person making the decision has power, even if the choice itself is an imposition. Second, studies show that simply offering a choice between two positive alternatives can increase the response rate to one of them. Meaning, if you ask your kids if they want fruit with dinner, the answer will be no more often than if you ask them to choose between apples and oranges.

Instructions for Designing with Forced Decisions

All games have decisions and choices; the question is when a forced decision will make a better behavioral game. Begin by outlining the major decisions that occur within your skill cycle, and think about how and when those decisions come about. Are key decisions being delayed or avoided? Are there new choices or tradeoffs you could be presenting to your players? Attempt to accelerate your game by forcing choices and note how this effects the dynamics of the experience so you can refine it later.

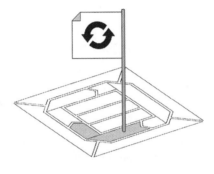

DATA

In Other Words: Information, Results, Indicators

Data is information in visible form. From raw numeric information to rich visualization, data reveal the hidden math behind our world. In any system, information related to our actions helps us make decisions and adjust our behavior.

A lack of data can lead to confusion about the state of things in a system, and can affect a person's play style. The less data we have, the more anxious we become; our sense of control erodes as we question our ability to succeed.

Case: Wii Fit

When the *Wii Fit* was announced, many people were skeptical that a glorified bathroom scale could become a popular video game. Today, it is recognized as the third best-selling console game in history. While this is surprising to some, from a behavioral games perspective it makes sense. Working out is an activity that is typically devoid of information. It's hard work, and you don't get anything to show for it until days or weeks later. The Wii system took a simple digital scale called the Wii Balance Board and turned it into a platform for dozens of exercise activities within the game. Your every move is converted into data, ratings, and feedback about how you're doing, and the system tells you exactly what you can do to reach your health goals.

Case: Ford Smart Gauge

Over the past few years several automakers have debuted feedback systems in their hybrid vehicles. These displays offer the driver a real-time sense of how their driving style is affecting gas mileage. Ford recently took this technology to the next level by creating the Smart Gauge with EcoGuide in partnership with famed design shops IDEO and Smart Design. Their system offers the driver performance data through a visual framework based on four principles: inform, enlighten, engage, and empower. One powerful visual in the system gives new meaning to the term *green driving*: when the car is operating efficiently an animation of vines and leaves sprouts from the right side of the screen. Accordingly, drivers report that they optimize their driving style within the first few weeks in the car.

Other Cases

> Chain restaurants in New York are required to display exact calorie counts for every item on their menus.

> ‣ Traffic signs that use radar to display the speed of passing drivers are cost-effective replacements for patrol cars.
> ‣ Designer Jin Kim's concept for a bathroom mirror makes brilliant use of embedded LEDs to show water consumption.
> ‣ *Guitar Hero* and *Rock Band* turn raw performance data into visual feedback so players can improve in real time.

Why Data Works

As we learned in our examination of the brain at play, our natural learning mechanism is very similar to that of the scientific method—we hypothesize, test, and interpret results to augment our theories. This process is how we make sense of the world around us. Without data and information we lack the ability to formulate new hypotheses, take new action, or refine our skills. Each bit of feedback is a novel and important experience to our brains, especially if the actions we're taking are deemed integral to achieving our goals.

Instructions for Designing with Data

Data should be employed in any instance where players are taking action and awaiting a system response. In designing a behavioral game, data and visual feedback are great places to start your creative process. Based on the desired behaviors that you're trying to encourage, think about what sorts of feedback would be most helpful or encouraging. What kind of information has never been available before? Now supply that information, in as close to real time as possible. Think about how to display that information in a simple and intuitive way. Remember though, that data can also backfire, as it may cause players to game the system, or reveal too much about the way the system works. Consider how your game can share key information but not reveal all its secrets.

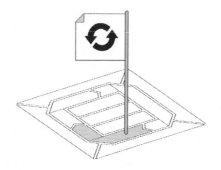

PROGRESS

In Other Words: Steps, Meters, Percentages

Progress is a specialized form of feedback in which a system plots a player's progress along a defined path or process. Anyone who has installed software on a home computer should be quite familiar with progress bars—those animated lines that indicate how long until the installation process is complete. Progress bars that show percentages for completion are a popular form, but any indication that a player is moving toward a goal counts.

One common complaint among Generation Y workers is that their progress in the workplace is so unclear. After putting in a solid year of long hours, are they 50 percent closer to a promotion? 90 percent? For these natural gamers, not knowing where they stand is the worst kind of limbo.

Case: LinkedIn

One of the most popular examples of progress on the web occurs during the profile creation process on LinkedIn. As you register, the site indicates what percentage of the setup process you've completed. The use of a progress bar and related messaging makes it clear that to get the most out of the site, you should complete your profile. The interface clearly lists the steps you should take, such as uploading a picture, adding past or present jobs, and listing your specialties. For many new users, the taunt of the progress bar is enough to encourage profile completion. As a result, LinkedIn is rumored to have a completion rate that is leagues better than other professional networks.

Case: Mint.com

Managing personal finances has always been a struggle of willpower and organization. Mint.com burst onto the scene in 2007 with a radically simplified approach to tracking personal finances online. Users can securely enter their bank and credit card information and the service automatically grabs and records purchases and deposits. What's more, the site files and categorizes purchases *automatically* according to budgets that users select. A clear visual progress bar for each line item in the budget shows users exactly how their spending is tracking against their goals.

Other Cases

> - Writer P. G. Wodehouse used to stick all the pages of a manuscript on his walls, near the ceiling if he loved them, near the floor if he didn't; rewriting the lowest pages until all of them touched the ceiling.
> - MiniCooper buyers can track the manufacturing and shipping progress of their custom-ordered Mini online.
> - Navigation systems in cars and planes display progress towards a destination, along with the time and distance remaining.
> - Shipping companies like FedEx and UPS offer detailed package tracking services that show exactly where a package is located.

Why Progress Works

Progress is a powerful indication that we're growing and developing. From an evolutionary perspective, it's advantageous to be addicted to progress—we never rest on our laurels. However, in many settings, progress is hard to detect, which often leads to demotivation. By making a goal apparent and showing us that we're moving, progress indicators add gas to our internal fire. Additionally, showing that we've completed some percentage of a process can lead to loss aversion when people consider leaving that endeavor. "Well, I've already gone this far, why stop now?"

Instructions for Designing with Progress

Using a progress indicator makes sense whenever you have a process or series of stages that you want your players to pursue. This is also ideal in situations where you don't want players to leave mid-process. Be sure that the progress is shown in a highly visual and highly visible manner. Progress can be communicated in terms of percentages, days remaining, or almost any unit of measurement, as long as an end goal is in sight. Consider confronting players with their current progress at regular intervals.

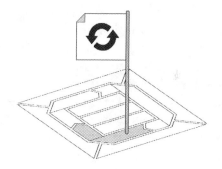

POINTS

In Other Words: Scores, Ratings, Grades

Points are a unit of measurement for performance—a specialized kind of data awarded within a game. Points give players a clear indication of what is valued by the system, and the relative importance of individual behaviors. In a point system, as the action unfolds, or at the conclusion of a session of action, points are awarded. Based on this, players will evaluate their performance and the performance of others. Points, at least from a game design perspective, are not exchangeable for anything of value inside or outside the game. In most sporting events, however, points are the sole means of determining the winner. There are points awarded by a system, and points awarded by other players (often referred to as "reputation"). Point totals are often referred to as scores, and can even be elevated to legend (e.g., world record for all-time home runs).

A lack of points can make individual actions seem less valuable, or disguise the actions that matter most. Points in any form tend to amplify or enable other elements like currency, levels, and competition.

Case: Points for Grades

Lee Sheldon, a professor at Indiana University, uses an experience points system in place of a traditional grading system in several of his classes. Students receive points for attending class and participating in the discussion, as well as group projects and tests. In this way, students see the semester as a cumulative experience, rather than a series of exams that can pull their letter grade up or down. While other professors are skeptical about the approach, Sheldon asserts that students are more engaged and active than ever. The points system has changed their sense of *faculty* by making every action count for something.

Case: Zeo Sleep Device

Dave Dickinson and his circle of friends at Brown University were hoping to get a better night's sleep. So they paired a sophisticated alarm clock with a lightweight headband capable of measuring brainwaves and the various stages of sleep (light, deep, REM, etc.). In doing so, they discovered that the stage of sleep you're in when you wake has a huge impact on how you feel. The resulting product, called Zeo, tracks your sleep as you rest, and waits for the optimal moment to wake you. Most important, the Zeo uses all the data it collects and a special algorithm to give you a rating of your sleep performance, called a "Z score." We spend over twenty years of our lives asleep, but the Z score presents an opportunity to evaluate the quality of that sleep objectively for the first time. Zeo users make lifestyle adjustments to optimize and improve their Z score, a score with no clear upper limit.

Other Cases

> Website ChoreWars.com allows users to band together with other members of their household and claim experience points for completing chores.
> Weight Watchers famously created a point system for making healthier choices with food.
> Health professionals created the BMI score as a smarter way to evaluate overall fitness beyond weight.
> Website HotorNot.com asks visitors to rate the attractiveness of other users on a 1–10 scale.

Why Points Work

Points have a magical effect on the brain. We see them as a reward, even when they're worthless, because they are a form of validation. Points represent an abstraction of value, and so we often act irrationally when points are in the mix. In one study, researchers found that people attempted to win an undesirable ice cream flavor, simply because it was associated with a higher score than the flavor they preferred. Keep in mind that since raw points don't translate into tangible rewards (although they can easily be turned into a currency), much of the success of a points system comes from the social status that points imply.

Instructions for Designing with Points

Points are great in any game that offers a variety of actions. When building a points system, determine what the possible actions are, and then how much each is worth. Think about how quickly you'll be able to award points to players, and whether an automated point system is necessary. Alternatively, consider that points often lead to competition and point-seeking behavior, so deploy them carefully and reevaluate often.

SENSATION

In Other Words: Stimulation, Motion, Touch

Good games make use of all of our senses, and being physical creatures, many of the most satisfying experiences we have involve sensation. Be it the rush of a roller coaster or the feeling of hitting a golf ball, these activities are fun by virtue of the *feelings* they bring out in us. Physical intensity can trigger the release of endorphins in the brain, which in turn create a pleasurable state of arousal. As a result, a sense of movement, vertigo, or any novel stimulus can quickly engage us. In terms of behavioral game design, we can assume that playing off any of our senses could represent powerful feedback. In some cases, sensation itself can be mimicked. Just *seeing* something associated with a physical sensation can trigger mirror neurons, suspension of disbelief, and all the feelings that you'd expect from the real thing. That's why simulators are so much fun.

Systems that lack sensation can feel flat and one-dimensional. Players may engage, but they'll never feel the sense of heightened emotion that comes from a richer sensory experience.

Case: Nissan Eco Pedal

One potential solution to the problem of inefficient driving habits comes from the engineers at Nissan, looking beyond just visual feedback to something more physical. The ECO Pedal system carefully monitors fuel consumption while the car is in motion and determines optimal rates of acceleration. If the driver tries to use excess pressure to accelerate in an inefficient way, the pedal pushes back (an ECO light on the dashboard also flashes), sending a subtle physical reminder to the driver: *you're wasting energy.* Of course, for safety reasons, the driver can always overpower the gentle resistance, but the message is clear. Studies by Nissan show a fuel savings of 5 to 10 percent depending on driving conditions.

Case: The Bubble Calendar

At my company, we operate in an environment with limited structure. Our employees come and go as they please, and set their hours based on meetings and obligations rather than an arbitrary corporate schedule. A couple of years ago, I stumbled upon something called a "bubble calendar" and ordered it for the office. This oversize wall calendar displays every day of the year, with a sheet of large bubble wrap laid over the entire thing, covering each date with a bubble. Understandably, when looking at the calendar, your immediate urge is to *pop all of those bubbles.* It's visceral. To make a behavioral game of it and give a nod to the dedicated folks that stay late, we added one rule at the office: the last one out gets to pop the bubble for that day. Silly, but surprisingly effective. For the entire year that calendar was in service, people took irrational pleasure in staying late and claiming their prize (this author included).

Other Cases

> 3D movies and video games are banking on the premise that seeing things in three dimensions will heighten the sensory experience.

- › Playing French or German music in a supermarket has been shown to influence the nationality of the wine being purchased, even if the music is too quiet to be consciously heard.
- › One participant in The Fun Theory created a doormat with an interactive surface that would play record-scratching sounds as people wiped their feet, to great effect.
- › Mobile phones vibrate and beep to alert us to new emails, calls, and texts—sensations we're now totally conditioned to notice.

Why Sensation Works

We like to feel good, and sensations that make us feel that way are highly sought after. From the satisfaction of popping a bubble to the exhilaration of sky diving, our sensory interactions with the world around us arouse our brains—releasing adrenaline and other neurotransmitters—and engage us in the moment.

Instructions for Designing with Sensation

Sensation works well when players need to be reinvigorated or refocused on the task at hand. To use sensation in a behavioral game, consider the environment and the kind of sensation that would be most surprising, satisfying, or exhilarating. Consider sight, sound, smell, taste, and touch. Remember that people interpret sensation differently, and have different thresholds for comfort, so choose something that will work across the board.

RECOGNITION

In Other Words: Achievements, Badges, Awards

Recognition is an acknowledgment that conveys our approval. Whether it be a blue ribbon, a badge, a plaque on the wall, or a pink Mary Kay Cadillac, public recognition is a powerful thing. While recognition can certainly come from the system itself, it is the sharing of that achievement that gives it its significance. We need to share our victories and be recognized by our peers. That's why gamers are constantly showing off their recent successes. In response, games have evolved to include instant replays and visible signs of past accomplishments. Xbox achievements grew into a social phenomenon on the back of this dynamic as well.

A lack of recognition can result in reduced motivation and a sense of isolation. As a social and tribal organism, we must translate our accomplishments back to the group and determine what they might mean for our status within it.

Case: Foursquare

In 2000, Dennis Crowley founded Dodgeball, a text message service that allowed friends to share their location with one another. When it was acquired by Google the service never really took off, and was ultimately absorbed by Google Latitude. Dennis left Google with a clear mission: build a better mousetrap. Foursquare burst onto the scene last year as an advanced location-based service, but it wasn't clear from day one what was going to drive adoption. This time Dennis and his partner Naveen Selvadurai put gaming into the mix, with points, badges, tips, friends, and status. Foursquare offered points for checking in at locations (and more points for new locations or multiple stops in one night), badges for exploratory achievements (checking in to three venues with photo booths earns a "photogenic" badge), and mayoral status (awarded for checking into a venue most often). If users earned enough points in a week, they'd rank on a citywide leaderboard. Competition ensued. Adding to this status-seeking dynamic, badges were prominently displayed on user profiles, hearkening back to the original genius of the Boy Scouts. The service took off and went from a few thousand members to over three million in less than eighteen months. Whether Foursquare's game mechanics prey on our compulsion to compete or actually engage us in something meaningful is dependent on one thing: is the service making us better? Time will tell.

Other Cases

> Alcoholics Anonymous recognizes periods of sobriety with special tokens in denominations ranging from twenty-four hours to one month, one year, and beyond.

> thredUp has brought game mechanics to clothing swaps, offering recognition to users by posting their names in a weekly leaderboard on the home page, in categories like "most stylish" and "super sender."

> The popular but often mismanaged tradition of recognizing an "employee of the month" is practiced at innumerable companies around the world.

> Those same global jet-setters who see new cities as levels view their passport stamps as badges of accomplishment.

Why Recognition Works

When other people in our social circle pay attention to us, our brains release dopamine and endorphins, signaling a reward. In nature, having the admiration and attention of others is a sure sign that we've done something significant and raised our standing with the tribe. An achievement alone is significant, but when coupled with some kind of token or symbol, and given in a public way, that achievement provides a deep satisfaction of our innate desire for status.

Instructions for Designing with Recognition

Although the token of recognition may be a badge or trophy, the public display or presentation of that award is extremely important, as we've covered. Think about the kinds of behavior and accomplishments you want to reward—they should be ones that you want to see repeated. Remember, recognition should stimulate further development, not stunt it by communicating a sense of completion. In this way, a Boy Scout merit badge is better than an Eagle Scout certificate. Consider that while players love to be recognized, they also like to offer praise to others. By building in mechanisms for reciprocation, you set everyone up to grow.

STATUS

In Other Words: Rank, Class, Reputation

Status is the manifestation of power and respect in a social group. It represents the kind of basic hierarchy that helps us create social order. Nearly everywhere you look, you'll see social status in action. The military calls it rank. Business calls it position or title. Students are defined by grade: eighth graders, ninth graders, and so on. Status comes in so many variations that it can be hard to recognize. But rest assured, whenever there is a hierarchy of experience, power, opportunity, or responsibility, you can be sure status is present. As you'd suspect, status and levels go hand in hand, but are distinct from each other. Levels refer to new challenges and areas within a system. Status refers to faculty, power, and reputation within a system, and among other players. Higher-status players get to do more, see more, and have more. In this way status and levels are symbiotic: the status or rank that players have achieved indicates the level they're currently exploring.

A lack of status among players can lead to confusion about roles and authority. It can also inhibit the spread of knowledge, as the players who know how to progress are harder to identify.

Case: Centurion Card

In the 1980s, urban legends about a black credit card with unmatched spending power were whispered from person to person, building up the belief that some astronomical level of wealth entitled certain people to a special level of service. Some of the possibly apocryphal purchases ascribed to the card included dispatching a team to collect sand from the Dead Sea for a school project, and locating, acquiring, and shipping the horse ridden by Kevin Costner in *Dances with Wolves* to a cardmember. Propelled by the strength of these rumors, American Express introduced the Centurion card in 1999. The card was invitation-only until 2006, and to this day requires applicants to meet a series of criteria not disclosed by American Express, but reported to include annual spending of over $250,000 per year and a $5,000 membership fee. In return, members get a dedicated concierge available by phone and access to parties, seats, reservations, and other perks not available to the common man. The "black card" as it is known in popular culture has been the subject of much speculation and desire, and is routinely referenced in rap songs and blog posts as the ultimate expression of status. With membership in the Centurion club now well documented, online rumors have moved on to referencing white and pearl cards that sit above Centurion—giving even the very wealthy a new level of status to shoot for.

Case: Flight Status

We know that frequent flier miles make an excellent point system and currency, but they also represent a case study in status. Each airline has its own levels of status, but across the board higher status means perks including: access to business and first-class lounges, reserving unoccupied adjacent seats, free or discounted upgrades, preference if a flight is oversold, and the ability to grant status to another person. Almost unbelievably, at certain elite statuses some airlines allow their best customers to bump existing ticketed passengers off sold-out flights. Airports and airlines make a big deal out of status on the whole, from the way they isolate first class (with a silly curtain) to the variety of "red carpet" clubs, and even separate boarding pathways. For anyone who flies more than a few times a year, this game has too many perks not to play.

Other Cases

› The developer community Stack Overflow uses reputation levels to indicate status and influence across the site.

› Empire Avenue is a virtual stock exchange that lets you buy and sell shares in *other people* based on their social influence online—if their status/influence goes up, you win.

› Academia is full of status cues, from degrees that are attached to your name (Ph.D., Esq., M.D.) to the notion of tenure.

› Yankee White clearance is a special kind of status in the government, which means that you have undergone the most rigorous background check available, and have access to certain high-profile jobs that demand loyalty.

Why Status Works

Status is part of our wiring as tribal animals. In the wild it's important to know where we stand. Status works because it offers us a kind of shorthand for cataloging the people and experiences around us. Once we know their level of status, we know a lot about what they can do for us, and how we should interact with them.

Instructions for Designing with Status

Use status when you're working on an activity in which power is an incentive. What is status is good for in your game? What rights or opportunities does it afford? Consider that upper limits on status make it about protecting the status quo rather than continued development. While a black belt in karate can look forward to becoming a grand master, a head nurse or public school teacher has effectively peaked, and may lose momentum and focus on protecting their turf as a result.

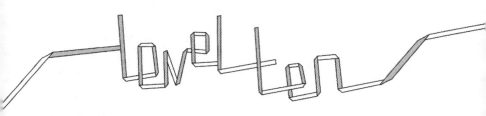

It's up to us. We've seen how games work from the inside out. We've explored how they make us better. And we've learned how a new breed of game, the behavioral game, can help us achieve our potential. But today we face global issues that go beyond our personal development. Unlike problems that we can solve with policy alone, these issues almost certainly require that we change our behavior at the individual and family level, because *we're* the problem.

Waste happens in *our* trash cans. Industrial food is supported by our decision to hit the drive-through instead of the farmers' market. Getting a better education for our kids means showing up at school and fighting a system built around standardized tests. In almost every case, it's a *grassroots* response that will result in maximum progress. The future of democracy is in voting with our dollars and decisions; the ballot is simply too passive.

The level of individual commitment and action we need is hard to inspire. Which begs the question, are documentaries and public service messages really the best way to address these issues? Is conversation enough? At least in the case of the green movement, the answer is no. While climate change has received an enormous amount of media coverage in the last few years, the vast majority of U.S. families still maintain roughly the same carbon footprint. This isn't all that surprising. We have households and businesses to run, and each of them is flush with daily challenges and hurdles to jump. Too often, our social responsibilities get lost in the daily grind.

I wonder if in addition to spreading the word, we could find opportunities to encourage the right choices without saying a thing. Could it be possible to attack these issues with behavioral games? Without question, these are complex issues requiring nuanced and complementary strategies. But there is *something* to the idea that we can use game dynamics to encourage different behavior around our most pressing challenges.

With all this in mind, it's clear that we need a generation of problem solvers in the worst way. As Jane McGonigal has routinely pointed out, our greatest natural resource may be the legions of gamers who are themselves masters in the art of working together to find solutions. I would add to that group the game designers and behavioral game designers who have yet to realize the full potential of their craft.

To say that the people who design games today are an *untapped resource* of behavioral insight is an understatement. Pitted against a real-world problem, any game designer worth their salt is able to draw from a treasure chest of psychological triggers and techniques that have the power to turn the issue on its head. They know how to think about and how to influence human behavior. To an experienced game designer, the thrust of this book is a woefully obvious message. But what is obvious to them is still novel to the vast majority of decision makers and leaders that shape our world.

Unfortunately, we don't all have our own game design experts to call upon when the people we lead feel bored, unmotivated, or unsure. The fact is, most of those experts are out there chasing the almighty dollar in the world of commercial video games. While we wait for more of them to join us back here in reality, we must begin to put their knowledge into practice, and gather new learnings of our own.

Great Power, Great Responsibility

Knowing what we do about the way games are designed, it's exciting to think about the impact this mindset could have on some of our most traditional institutions. Everything from the public school system to the department of motor vehicles could use a radical overhaul based on the principles of behavioral game design—which are essentially the principles of attention and engagement. Can you imagine a world where our most basic activities are even half as enjoyable as our favorite games? Where every ounce of learning is *due* to play rather than at its expense? That world can be made real, one game at a time.

Right now, Katie Salen and her co-conspirators in the world of education are giving us a free preview. Their radical new school, Quest to Learn, is taking a game-centric approach to education, from inside the New York City public school system. At *this* school, 145 sixth and seventh graders spend their days in a digitally enabled environment where subjects are blurred into classes with names like Codeworlds (a hybrid of math and English) that use game mechanics, narrative fantasy, and a heavy dose of interaction and technology to keep students engaged. It's too early to say how this approach will affect future performance but seeing new world skills front and center in the classroom is an encouraging sign.

Given how engaging and influential game-driven environments like Quest to Learn could be, it's easy to get excited about the possibilities without considering the potential consequences of experiments that focus on influencing or changing behavior. We are playing with powerful forces here—some of the oldest and most primal circuitry in our brains. We have a responsibility to consider what behaviors we're encouraging, who benefits if we're successful, and what's at stake if our games create adverse results. As Yoda once said, "With great power comes great responsibility."

Games can be used to manipulate and persuade—to turn our

compulsions and social obligations against us in order to feed a bottom line. And there will be plenty of pressure to do just that in the months and years to come. Yet lasting and meaningful engagement comes not from repetitive and compulsive experiences, but from skills-based play that helps us achieve our potential as individuals *and* organizations. We can't ignore the long-term role of play in favor of a frenzy of misguided game mechanics.

The fact is, taking on the role of a behavioral game designer is different from designing other games; a behavioral game never "ships." When a game designer finishes a title, that experience is left in the hands of its players. As behavioral game designers, when launching something new we must wait and watch closely. Like a sound engineer, our job is ever vigilant, and when things don't sound quite right, we tweak the dials.

Behavioral game design is as much an art as it is a science. We must respect the complexity of our consciousness, and tread carefully as we begin to exert our influence over it. Games have the power to teach us, not just about *imaginary* worlds, but about the *real* world and our role in shaping it. Every time we learn something new in a game, we also learn something new about ourselves.

Whether you're a behavioral economist, a business manager, a student, a teacher, a politician, a stay-at-home parent, or an entrepreneur, there is a battle being waged that will determine the kind of world we live in. It's a battle for our hearts and minds. Some will fight with laws. Others with policies and interoffice memos. A handful will do battle using marketing. And many more will simply sit on the sidelines and watch, unsure of how they can help. I believe that we can fight the status quo with play, if we weave it into the fabric of our lives so gracefully that it's indistinguishable from the systems we've come to rely on: business, academia, philanthropy, and any other form of community.

It's time for *us* to take action to fix the poorly structured systems and organizations that are compounding our boredom and apathy, and limiting our potential for growth. You can help. Propose, design, share, and discuss behavioral games with the rest of us on the *Game Frame* website. As a community we can inspire and challenge one another, refining a collective approach as we move toward a brighter future. My challenge to you is simple: I believe that a million behavioral games could change everything, but they must be imagined and realized soon.

Play is at the heart of what it means to be human. Within each of us is a confident, driven, ever-learning hero who loves a good game. It's time for these heros to emerge. Game on.

APPENDIX
Putting It into Practice

The best way to build your skills as a behavioral game designer is to put them to use. To that end, I've designed a series of four exercises that will let you stretch your wings with a safety net. Included with each exercise is basic information about the challenge at hand, followed by a partially completed Game Frame. It's your job to fill out the blank spaces and describe your skill cycle(s) in order to complete the game.

On the *Game Frame* website you can enter your solution, look at other solutions from the community, and see my complete Game Frame and skill cycle(s) for each scenario. Remember there are no wrong answers here, only better and better behavioral games!

Scenario One: Cab Chaos

A local cab company has decided that it's time to stand out from the competition. One of the most common complaints from customers is that cab drivers are erratic and aggressive, making the ride experience anxious and unpleasant. This driving behavior is due to incentives already in place. The drivers get to start their meters with a minimum fare of a couple dollars preloaded, making a higher number of passengers more desirable than one long fare. Additionally, passengers want to get to their destination as quickly *and* safely as possible, a tension drivers resolve by focusing on speed.

Design a behavioral game to increase the safety and quality of the ride, without compromising overall fares.

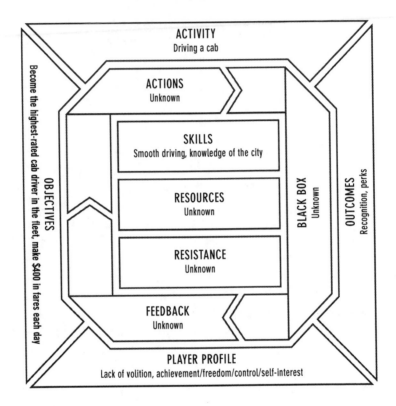

Scenario Two: Use the Force

A national technology company that sells products and services to other businesses is having trouble with its sales force. The head of sales has decided that two skills are key to success across the entire team: preparation and follow-through. He believes that if his salespeople prepare for sales meetings ahead of time, and follow up regularly afterward, results will improve dramatically.

Design a behavioral game to encourage and improve preparation and follow-through across the salesforce.

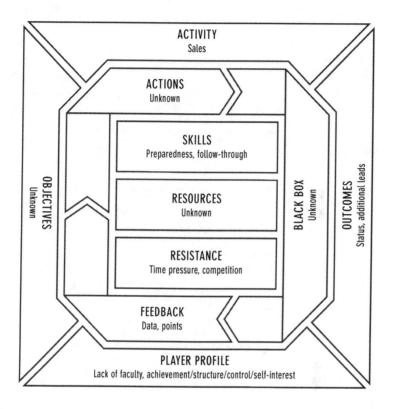

Scenario Three: What's Cooking

You've decided that it's time to step up your skills as an amateur chef. You fancy yourself a decent cook but want to be more inventive—able to make something delicious with whatever is on hand. However, you often come home tired from a day of work, and so you tend to order in or cook the usual quick recipes.

Design a behavioral game that will help you take your cuisine to the next level and encourage innovation.

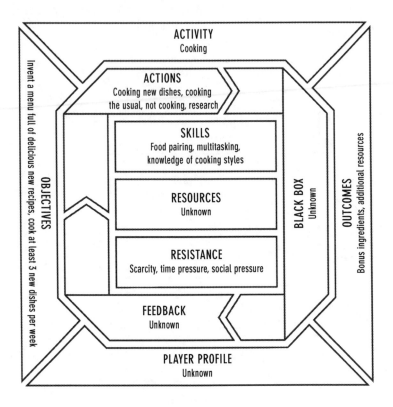

Scenario Four: The Short Stay

A retail bookstore is getting plenty of foot traffic, but visitors are leaving the bookstore after only a few minutes, and often with no purchases. Store managers are convinced that if they can get people to spend more time browsing in the store, they'll see sales improve.

Design a behavioral game that will encourage customers to browse the store more fully.

APPENDIX

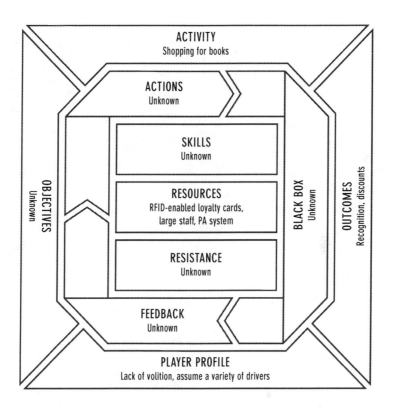

ACTIVITY
Shopping for books

ACTIONS
Unknown

SKILLS
Unknown

RESOURCES
RFID-enabled loyalty cards,
large staff, PA system

RESISTANCE
Unknown

FEEDBACK
Unknown

OBJECTIVES
Unknown

BLACK BOX
Unknown

OUTCOMES
Recognition, discounts

PLAYER PROFILE
Lack of volition, assume a variety of drivers

ACKNOWLEDGMENTS

Writing a book about a movement that has only just begun is an uphill climb. The notion that games have lessons to teach us about how our minds work, and that they can reshape the world around us, is not new, just underdeveloped. The convergence of the game world and the real world can only be understood through the combined perspective of many fields. Fortunately for me, thought leaders from those disciplines have been at this for a while. Over the course of this project I was fortunate enough to find and (hopefully) grok several dozen books, hundreds of blogs, and thousands of tweets from game-loving luminaries around the world. First and foremost, let me just say that Mihaly Csikszentmihalyi is ten steps ahead of us. His work on the psychology of optimal experience is referenced in nearly every book on games that I've seen. In fact, it became a running joke to see how many pages I could flip before *Flow* was cited. I was also heavily influenced by the amazing work of Katie Salen, Eric Zimmerman, Jesse Schell, Jane McGonigal, Ian Bogost, Daniel Cook, Amy Jo Kim, Raph Koster, Marc Prensky, Stuart Brown, James Paul Gee, Edward Castronova, Steven Johnson, Richard Thaler, Cass Sunstein, Dan Ariely, Sebastian Deterding, and my new friends at Natron Baxter: Nathan Verrill and Matthew Jenson. Gang, this is your party—I'm just spiking the punch bowl.

My team at Undercurrent is like nothing the world has ever seen. Getting to work alongside people of this caliber and character is a humbling experience. Without the technical advice of game enthusiast and UCer Eric Tabone, I would have undoubtedly ruined this book for hardcore gamers. Fellow UCers Lucy Blair and Brandi Bullard were unflinching in their willingness to help me do the dirty work behind this book. My partners in Undercurrent, Josh Spear and Rob Schuham, are incredible co-conspirators, and patiently supported me as I attempted the plate-spinning act of building a business and writing a book at the same time. And of course, a big gong hit to the rest of my team: Alex, Amy, Ana, Andrew A., Andrew D., Clay, Gautam, Jim, Joe, Johanna, Jonathan, Lauren, Marisa, Matthew, Mike, Rachel, Sam, Vladimir, and any future members of the UC family.

My research assistant Paula Cizek was a total rock star in the early days of this project, filling my head with all the right ingredients to bake something new. Scott Belsky was kind enough to go through the publishing process almost a year ahead of me, and has shared many lessons kindly and freely. Super agent Meg Thompson was undoubtedly the first person to see the big picture here, and turned out to be a wonderful tour guide to the world of publishing (a somewhat strange place to a digital guy like me). Larry, Meg, and the rest of the team at LJK Literary Management continue to be incredibly supportive partners in crime. I owe a big thank-you to my editor Amber Qureshi, who made this process more fluid than I ever thought it could be. She and the entire team at Free Press have been committed to doing this right from day one. I'm also indebted to design wunderkind Owen Gildersleeve, who stepped in at the last minute to make this book more than a pile of words.

I'm very fortunate to come from a family that knows how to play. My mother Barb makes the rest of us look downright serious by making her living teaching theater to teenagers. Her love of imaginative play has touched the lives of more people than anyone I know. She is my hero. Thanks to my brother Ben I finally understand why sports are so important. If you follow that world at all, you'll be hearing from him soon. I'm also grateful to my dad Pete for telling me to be the best I can be every day for a decade. He and his wife Kelly shared many dinner conversations with me that stretched and sharpened the thinking reflected in

ACKNOWLEDGMENTS

this book. A special thanks to my grandparents for showing me the joy of playing ping-pong and "spit" when I was just knee-high. And a sincere thanks to the rest of my clan (including my new in-laws Becky, Chris, and Zach) for your ongoing love and support.

Although it's not nearly enough, a massive thank-you to my wife Britt, who stuck with me while I disappeared for the better part of a year to write this book. Her edits, counsel, and support for this project truly made it what you hold in your hands.

Finally, ten bonus points to all the lifelong players out there who strive to find the fun in everything. You make the mundane magical.

NOTES

Level One

Josh Knowles, "Add Some XBOX to Your UX." *Auscillate*, <http://auscillate.com/writing/xbox_ux>.

Raph Koster, *A Theory of Fun for Game Design* (Scottsdale: Paraglyph Press, 2005), p. 28.

"Montessori method," <http://www.wikipedia.org/wiki/Montessori_method>.

Mihaly Csikszentmihalyi, *Flow: The Psychology of Optimal Experience* (New York: HarperCollins, 1991), pp. 74–75.

Joseph Campbell, *The Power of Myth* (Anchor Books, 1991).

Level Two

Street Wars, <http://www.streetwars.net/>

J. C. Herz, *Joystick Nation: How Videogames Ate Our Quarters, Won Our Hearts, and Rewired Our Minds* (Boston: Little, Brown, 1997), p. 50.

"2009 U.S. Video Game Industry and PC Game Software Retail Sales Reach $20.2 Billion," *NPD.com.* 01 14 2010. <http://www.npd.com/press/releases/press_100114.html>.

Paul Bond, "Growth in Gaming Still On," *AdWeek* 06 16 2009. <http://www.adweek.com/aw/content_display/data-center/research/e3iec-fa450e38f03b771917c5b71775f531>.

"Grand Theft Auto (series)." <http://en.wikipedia.org/wiki/Grand_Theft_Auto_(series)>.

Brendan Sinclair, "MS: 17.7 million 360s sold," *GameSpot.com* 01 03 2008. <http://www.gamespot.com/news/6184291.html>.

Tom Ivan, "Call of Duty Series Tops 55 Million Sales," *EDGE* 11 27 2009. <http://www.next-gen.biz/news/call-of-duty-series-tops-55-million-sales>.

NOTES

Dean Takahashi, "That screeching sound? U.S. video game industry sales decline in 2009," *GamesBeat* 01 14 2010. <http://games.venturebeat.com/2010/01/14/that-screeching-sound-u-s-video-game-industry-sales-decline-in-2009/>.

J. Leighton Read and Byron Reeves, *Total Engagement: Using Games and Virtual Worlds to Change the Way People Work and Businesses Compete* (Boston: Harvard Business Press, 2009), p. 20.

"Electronic Arts Acquires Playfish," *playfish.com* 09 11 2009. <http://www.playfish.com/press_releases/?release=09_11_2009l>

Dustin Quillen, "World of Warcraft Tops 11.5 Million Subscribers," *1Up.com* 12 23 2008. <http://www.1up.com/news/world-warcraft-tops-115-million>.

"Greatest freak out ever," 05 05 2009. <http://www.youtube.com/watch?v=YersIyzsOpc>.

Matthew Ingram, "Average Social Gamer Is a 43-Year-Old Woman," *GigaOM* 02 17 2010. <http://gigaom.com/2010/02/17/average-social-gamer-is-a-43-year-old-woman/>.

Roger Caillois, *Man, Play, and Games* (Urbana: University of Illinois Press, 2001), pp. 37–41, 57–67.

Laura Dabbish and Luis von Ahn, "Designing Games with a Purpose," *Communications of the ACM* 51.9 (2008): 58.

Jane McGonigal, "Gaming can make a better world," TED2010, February 2010. <http://www.ted.com/talks/jane_mcgonigal_gaming_can_make_a_better_world.html>.

Eric Hagerman, "Point. Click. Kill: Inside The Air Force's Frantic Unmanned Reinvention," *Popular Science* 08 18 2009. <http://www.popsci.com/drones>.

Gail E. Hawisher and Cynthia L. Selfe, *Literate Lives in the Information Age: Narratives of Literacy from the United States* (Lawrence Erlbaum Associates, 2004), p. 3.

John C. Beck and Mitchell Wade, *The Kids Are Alright: How the Gamer Generation Is Changing the Workplace* (Boston: Harvard Business School Press, 2006), pp. 35, 161

Mark Prensky, *Digital Game-Based Learning* (St. Paul: Paragon House, 2001), p. 45.

Ryan Fleming, "Study Claims Cognitive Functions Increased Through Casual Gaming," *Digital Trends* 05 26 2010. <http://www.digitaltrends.com/gaming/study-claims-cognitive-functions-increased-through-casual-gaming/>

Douglas A. Gentile, "Video Games Affect the Brain—For Better and

NOTES

Worse," Dana Foundation 07 23 2009. <http://www.dana.org/news/cerebrum/detail.aspx?id=22800>.

Carolyn Abraham, "Better Living Through Video Games?" *The Globe and Mail* 04 05 2009. <http://www.theglobeandmail.com/news/technology/science/article812922.ece>.

Steven Johnson, "Your Brain on Video Games," *DISCOVER Magazine* 07 24 2005. <http://discovermagazine.com/2005/jul/brain-on-video-games>.

"Neuroplasticity." <http://en.wikipedia.org/wiki/Neuroplasticity>.

Level Three

"Opioids." <http://en.wikipedia.org/wiki/Opioids>.

"Neurotransmitter." <http://en.wikipedia.org/wiki/Neurotransmitter>.

Helen Philips, "Instant Expert: The Human Brain," *NewScientist.com* 09 04 2006. <http://www.newscientist.com/article/dn9969>.

Emily Yoffe, "Seeking: How the Brain Hard-Wires Us to Love Google, Twitter and Texting," *Slate.com* 08 12 2009. <http://www.slate.com/id/2224932/pagenum/all/>.

Daniel R. Hawes, "When We Want Something More Although We Like It Less," *PsychologyToday.com* 02 22 2010. <http://www.psychologytoday.com/blog/evolved-primate/201002/when-we-want-something-more-although-we-it-less>.

Steven Johnson, *Everything Bad Is Good for You: How Today's Popular Culture Is Actually Making Us Smarter* (New York: Riverhead Books), p. 34.

Jaak Panksepp, *Affective Neuroscience: The Foundations of Human and Animal Emotions* (New York: Oxford University Press, 1998), pp. 54, 144, 280.

Stuart Brown, with Christopher Vaughan, *Play: How It Shapes the Brain, Opens the Imagination, and Invigorates the Soul* (New York: Avery, 2009), p. 33.

Jeff Hawkins, with Sandra Blakeslee, *On Intelligence: How a New Understanding of the Brain Will Lead to the Creation of Truly Intelligent Machines* (New York: Owl Books, 2004).

James Paul Gee, *Good Video Games + Good Learning* (New York: Peter Lang, 2008), p. 81.

———*Situated Language and Learning: A Critique of Traditional Schooling* (New York: Routledge, 2004), p. 71.

J. Huizinga, *Homo Ludens: A Study of the Play-Element in Culture* (Abingdon: Routledge, 1949), pp. 1, 13.

NOTES

Katie Salen and Eric Zimmerman, *Rules of Play: Game Design Fundamentals* (Cambridge: MIT Press, 2004), p. 304.

A. H. Maslow, "A Theory of Human Motivation," *Psychological Review* 50 (1943): 370–396.

Dale Carnegie, *How to Win Friends and Influence People* (New York: Simon & Schuster, 1936), p. 71.

Peter Gray, "Chasing Games and Sports: Why Do We Like to Be Chased?" *Psychology Today* 11 05 2008. <http://www.psychologytoday.com/blog/freedom-learn/200811/chasing-games-and-sports-why-do-we-be-chased>

Karlin Lillington, "Who Says Science Can't Be Fun?" *Wired.com* 01 16 2003. <http://www.wired.com/gaming/gamingreviews/news/2003/01/57232>

Level Four

Steven Johnson, *Everything Bad Is Good for You: How Today's Popular Culture Is Actually Making Us Smarter* (New York: Riverhead Books, 2005), p. 37.

Jane McGonigal, "Gaming Can Make a Better World," TED2010, February 2010. <http://www.ted.com/talks/jane_mcgonigal_gaming_can_make_a_better_world.html>.

David Edery and Ethan Mollick, *Changing the Game: How Video Games Are Transforming the Future of Business* (Upper Saddle River, NJ: FT Press, 2009), p. 5.

Katie Salen and Eric Zimmerman, *Rules of Play: Game Design Fundamentals* (Cambridge, MA: MIT Press, 2004), p. 80.

"Suspension of disbelief." <http://en.wikipedia.org/wiki/Suspension_of_disbelief>.

J. Huizinga, *Homo Ludens: A Study of the Play-Element in Culture* (Abingdon: Routledge, 1949), p. 77.

Garrison Keillor, *The Prairie Home Companion*.

"Illusory Superiority." <http://en.wikipedia.org/wiki/Illusory_superiority>.

David Dunning, Joyce Ehrlinger, Kerri Johnson, and Justin Kruger, "Why People Fail to Recognize Their Own Incompetence," *Current Directions in Psychological Science* 12:3 (2003): 83–87.

"Collectivist and individualist cultures." <http://psychology.wikia.com/wiki/Collectivist_and_individualist_cultures>.

"Optimism bias." <http://en.wikipedia.org/wiki/Optimism_bias>.

NOTES

James Paul Gee, *Good Video Games + Good Learning* (New York: Peter Lang, 2008), p. 142.

Johnson, *Everything Bad Is Good For You*, p. 147.

Steven Poole, *Trigger Happy: Videogames and the Entertainment Revolution* (New York: Arcade Publishing, 2000), p. 172.

Teresa Amabile, and Steven Kramer, "The HBR List: Breakthrough Ideas for 2010, 1: What Really Motivates Workers," *Harvard Business Review* 01 2010. <http://hbr.org/2010/01/the-hbr-list-breakthrough-ideas-for-2010/ar/1>

Edward Castronova, *Exodus to the Virtual World: How Online Fun Is Changing Reality* (New York: Palgrave Macmillan, 2007), p. 28.

I. G. Collin, "Irrational Behavior Episode 5: What Are We Afraid Of," *Irrational Games* 05 03 2010. <http://irrationalgames.com/insider/irrational-behavior-episode-5/>.

Simon Grondin, and Simon Tobin, "Video Games and the Perception of Very Long Durations by Adolescents," *Computers in Human Behavior* 25.2 (2009): 554–9.

Aaron M. Sackett, Tom Meyvis, Leif D. Nelson, Benjamin A. Converse, and Anna L. Sackett, "You're Having Fun When Time Flies: The Hedonic Consequences of Subjective Time Progression," *Psychological Science* 21.1 (2010): 111–117.

Eliza Strickland, "Heightened by Halo: First-Person Video Games Are Good for Your Vision," *Discover Magazine Blog 80beats* 03 30 2009. <http://blogs.discovermagazine.com/80beats/2009/03/30/hello-halo-first-person-video-games-are-good-for-your-eyesight/>

Ewen Callaway, "Video Game Conditioning Spills Over into Real Life." *New Scientist.com* 01 27 2009. <http://www.newscientist.com/article/dn16493-video-game-conditioning-spills-over-into-real-life.html>

John C. Beck and Mitchell Wade, *The Kids Are Alright: How the Gamer Generation Is Changing the Workplace* (Boston: Harvard Business School Press, 2006), p. 84.

Level Five

<http://fold.it/portal/>.

John Timmer, "Gamers Beat Algorithms at Finding Protein Structures." *ars technica* 08 04 2010. <http://arstechnica.com/science/news/2010/08/gamers-beat-algorithms-for-finding-protein-structures.ars>.

Ian Bogost, *Persuasive Games: The Expressive Power of Videogames* (Cambridge, MA: MIT Press, 2007), pp. 279–282.

NOTES

Ian Ayres, *Super Crunchers* (New York: Random House, 2008), p. 1.

Gary Wolf, "The Data-Driven Life," *New York Times* 04 28 2010. <http://www.nytimes.com/2010/05/02/magazine/02self-measurement-t.html?pagewanted=all>.

Helen Fisher, "Biology: Your Brain in Love," *Time* 01 19 2004. <http://www.time.com/time/magazine/article/0,9171,993160-3,00.html>

"Jerk-O-Meter Rates Phone Chatter," *Wired.com* 08 11 2005. <http://www.wired.com/techbiz/media/news/2005/08/68502>

Edward Castronova, *Exodus to the Virtual World: How Online Fun Is Changing Reality* (New York: Palgrave Macmillan, 2007), p. 175.

Jesse Schell, "Design Outside the Box," DICE 2010, February 2010. <http://g4tv.com/videos/44277/dice-2010-design-outside-the-box-presentation/>

"Brain-computer interface." <http://en.wikipedia.org/wiki/Brain%E2%80%93computer_interface>.

NeuroSky. <http://company.neurosky.com/products/>.

Emotiv. <http://www.emotiv.com/>.

"Emotiv Systems." <http://en.wikipedia.org/wiki/Emotiv_Systems>.

Dave Eyvazzadeh, "Mind Power Moves Toyota Wheelchair," *Wired.com* 06 29 2009. <http://www.wired.com/autopia/2009/06/toyota-wheelchair/>.

"Thought-controlled wheelchair in Japan." 06 29 2009. <http://www.youtube.com/watch?v=1VPY1d2t_FE>.

Level Six

Mark R. Lepper, David Greene, and Richard E. Nisbett, "Undermining Children's Intrinsic Interest with Extrinsic Reward: A Test of the 'Overjustification' Hypothesis," *Journal of Personality and Social Psychology* 28:1 (1973): 129–137.

"Overjustification effect." <http://en.wikipedia.org/wiki/Overjustification_effect>.

Mihaly Csikszentmihalyi, *Flow: The Psychology of Optimal Experience* (New York: HarperCollins, 1991), pp. 83–86.

"Reversal theory." <http://en.wikipedia.org/wiki/Reversal_theory>

Ian Bogost, "Persuasive Games: Shell Games," *Gamasutra* 03 03 2010. <http://www.gamasutra.com/view/feature/4294/persuasive_games_shell_games.php?page=2>.

"Edward Thorndike." <http://en.wikipedia.org/wiki/Edward_Thorndike>.

"Operant conditioning." <http://en.wikipedia.org/wiki/Operant_conditioning>.

NOTES

"Behavioral economics." <http://en.wikipedia.org/wiki/Behavioral_economics>.

"Endowment effect." <http://en.wikipedia.org/wiki/Endowment_effect>

Dan Ariely, *Predictably Irrational: The Hidden Forces That Shape Our Decisions* (New York: HarperCollins, 2010).

Cass Sunstein and Richard Thaler, *Nudge* (Caravan, 2008), pp. 5, 11, 155, 180–181.

"Piano Staircase," *TheFunTheory.com 09 22 2009.* <http://www.thefuntheory.com/piano-staircase>.

"Bottle Bank Arcade Machine," *TheFunTheory.com* 10 16 2009. <http://www.thefuntheory.com/bottle-bank-arcade-machine>.

Level Seven

Nike+ statistics, <http://nikerunning.nike.com>.

Andre Agassi, *Open: An Autobiography* (First Vintage Books, 2010), pp. 26–29.

Amy Jo Kim, "MetaGame Design: Reward Systems That Drive Engagement." Slideshare. <http://www.slideshare.net/amyjokim/metagame-design-3383058>.

Forgotten Works. <http://www.forgottenworks.org/quote_Dirac.html>.

"Introduction to Merit Badges." <http://www.scouting.org/scoutsource/BoyScouts/AdvancementandAwards/MeritBadges.aspx>.

Daniel Cook, "Ribbon Hero Turns Learning Office into a Game," *Lost Garden* 01 19 2010. <http://www.lostgarden.com/2010/01/ribbon-hero-turns-learning-office-into.html>.

Daniel Cook, "The Chemistry of Game Design," *Gamasutra* 07 19 2007. <http://www.gamasutra.com/view/feature/1524/the_chemistry_of_game_design.php?page=2>.

Level Eight

"Reversal theory." <http://en.wikipedia.org/wiki/Reversal_theory>.

Level Nine

Targets

<http://www.kickstarter.com/>.

Sunstein, Cass and Richard Thaler. *Nudge* (Caravan, 2008), p.4.

NOTES

"Heart rate." <http://en.wikipedia.org/wiki/Heart_rate>

Time Staff, "The World's Most Influential Person Is . . ." *Time.com* 04 27 2009. <http://www.time.com/time/arts/article/0,8599,1894028,00. html>.

Competition

Peter Bregman, "How to Make Solving Problems Fun," *Harvard Business Review* 09 15 2009. <http://blogs.hbr.org/bregman/2009/09/how-to-make-solving-problems-f.html>.

<http://www.nikegrid.com/>.

Steve Booth-Butterfield, "Skateboards, Hot Chicks, and Performance." *PsychologyToday.com* 01 06 2010. <http://www.psychologytoday.com/blog/persuade-me/201001/skateboards-hot-chicks-and-performance>.

Chance

<https://reservations.momofuku.com/>.

Martha Lagace, "Innovative Ways to Encourage Personal Savings," *Harvard Business School Working Knowledge* 06 23 2008. <http://hbswk.hbs.edu/item/5908.html>.

M. G., Siegler "Button: An iPhone Game That Just May Make You Better at Your Job," *TechCrunch* 08 31 2009. <http://techcrunch.com/2009/08/31/button-an-iphone-game-that-just-may-make-you-better-at-your-job/>.

Time Pressure

Dennis Crowley, *The Teenorama* 11 28 2009. <http://dpstyles.tumblr.com/post/260890668/screenshot-from-a-checkout-terminal-at-target>.

Scarcity

Merlin Mann, "Meeting Tokens, for Creating Time Scarcity," *43 Folders* 10 19 2007. <http://www.43folders.com/2007/10/19/meeting-tokens-scarcity>.

NOTES

Puzzles

Stefanie Olsen, "Google recruits eggheads with mystery billboard," *CNet. com* 07 09 2004. <http://news.cnet.com/Google-recruits-eggheads-with-mystery-billboard/2100–1023_3-5263941.html>.
"Oulipo." <http://en.wikipedia.org/wiki/Oulipo>.
<http://bookoven.com/>.

Social Pressure

<http://www.ted.com>.
Matthew J. Salganik and Duncan J. Watts. "Leading the Herd Astray: An Experimental Study of Self-fulfilling Prophecies in an Artificial Cultural Market," *Social Psychology Quarterly* 71 (2008): 338–355.
<http://www.facebook.com/MafiaWars>.
<http://socialworkout.com/>.

Teamwork

<http://openideo.com/>.
<http://www.odysseyofthemind.com/>.
<http://www.quirky.com>.

Currency

"Skee ball." <http://en.wikipedia.org/wiki/Skee_ball>.
Attent: <http://www.seriosity.com/products.html>.
"McDonald's Monopoly." <http://en.wikipedia.org/wiki/McDonald%27s_Monopoly>.

Renewal

"Take a shower to boost your employee productivity," *Employee Productivity* 05 20 2009. <http://www.employee-productivity.com/2009/05/take-a-shower-to-boost-your-employee-productivity/>.
Gizmodo Staff, "M.I.T. Ushers in Biking 2.0 with Copenhagen Wheel." *FastCompany.com* 12 16 2009. <http://www.fastcompany.com/blog/gizmodo-staff/gizmodo/mit-ushers-biking-20-copenhagen-wheel-bicycles>.

NOTES

Forced Decisions

J. Leighton Read and Byron Reeves, *Total Engagement: Using Games and Virtual Worlds to Change the Way People Work and Businesses Compete* (Boston: Harvard Business Press, 2009), pp. 213–15.

Jim Rohner, "Video Based Interactive Game 'How to Pick Up Girls' Shows Glimmer, Gets Laughs," *JawboneTV* 08 19 2009. <http://www.jawbone.tv/index.php?option=com_content&task=view&id=160>.

Data

"Wii Fit." <http://en.wikipedia.org/wiki/Wii_Fit>.

Alissa Walker, "Ford's SmartGauge Improves Fuel Efficiency Through Better Instrument Design," *FastCompany* 03 18 2009. <http://www.fastcompany.com/blog/alissa-walker/designerati/fords-smartgauge-helps-hybrid-drivers-increase-mileage-better-instrum>.

Jaymi Heimbuch, "Bathroom Mirror Shows Water Consumption in LEDs As You Wash Your Face," *TreeHugger.com* 01 05 2010. <http://www.treehugger.com/files/2010/01/bathroom-mirror-shows-water-consumption-in-colorful-leds-as-you-wash-your-face.php>.

Progress

<http://ask.metafilter.com/44315/Famous-Writing-Habits>.

Points

Amor Toor, "Prof Subs Grades for Experience Points, Presentations with Quests," *Switched* 03 26 2010. <http://www.switched.com/2010/03/26/prof-subs-grades-for-experience-points-presentations-with-quest/>.

Zeo About Us. <http://www.myzeo.com/pages/48_about_us.cfm>.

Sensation

Antuan Goodwin, "Nissan't ECO Pedal drives you to fuel efficiency," *CNet* 08 04 2008. <http://reviews.cnet.com/8301-13746_7-10005857-48.html>.

<http://www.perpetualkid.com/2010-bubble-calendar.aspx>.

Adrian C. North, David J. Hargreaves, and Jennifer McKendrick. "The

NOTES

Influence of In-Store Music on Wine Selections." *Journal of Applied Psychology 84: (1999)*: 271–276.
<http://www.funtheory.com>.

Recognition

<http://www.thredup.com/>.

Status

"Black American Express Card," *Snopes.com.* <http://www.snopes.com/business/bank/blackcard.asp>.
<http://stackoverflow.com/>.
<http://empireavenue.com/>.
"Yankee White." <http://en.wikipedia.org/wiki/Yankee_White>.

Level Ten

Sara Corbett, "Learning by Playing: Video Games in the Classroom," *New York Times Magazine* 09 15 2010. <http://www.nytimes.com/2010/09/19/magazine/19video-t.html>.

INDEX

INDEX

INDEX

INDEX

Evolutionary psychology, 30–31, 39, 152

Exodus to the Virtual World (Castronova), 45, 57–58

Extinction, 70

Facebook, 15, 16, 53, 94, 130

Faculty, 6, 8, 36, 89, 90, 132, 134, 139, 154

    lack of, 2, 3, 81

FarmVille, 15, 16

FedEx, 152

Feedback, xii, 8, 73, 83

    in behavioral game design, 94, 97, 110, 111, 150, 151

Fermat, Pierre de, 119

Final Fantasy XI, 67

Flow, 6–9, 25–26, 47, 122, 123

Flow (Csikszentmihalyi), 6, 66

Flynn effect, 43

Foldit, 52

Follow-through, 1

Football, 31

Forced decisions, in behavioral game design, 145–148

Ford Smart Gauge, 149

Forman, Charles, 141

4chan.org, 113

Foursquare, 13, 159–160

43Folders.com, 124

Freedom versus structure, 89, 99

Frequent flier miles, 141, 163

Frogger, 11

Fun, 2. *See also* Games; Play

    hard fun, 31

    learning and, 28

    play as, 30

Fun Theory, The, 74–75, 158

Gamasutra.com, 67

Gambling, 15, 119

Game Frame. *See* Behavioral game design

Game Frame website, 169, 171

Gamepocalypse, 58–59

Games, xiii

    alternate reality games (ARGs), 13–14

    behavioral. *See* Behavioral games; Behavioral game design

    blending into lives, 13

    brain chemistry and, 21, 23–26

    brain-computer interfaces (BCI), 60–61

    business of, 14–15

    cognitive changes and, 48–49

    in contrast to reward systems, 3

    control and, 5, 6, 43

    definitions of, 34–36

    demographics of gamers, 17

    designing. *See* Behavioral game design

    epic win, 34

    fear and, 45–46

    in future, 51–61, 63–75

    gadgetry and, 18–19

    gaming virtuosos, 19

    glory and, 46

    golden age of, 12–13

    grinding and, 67–68

    heroes and, 8–9, 41, 46, 49

    interdependence of culture and, 17–18

    jobs and, 19–20, 57–58

    magic circle and, 36–37, 81

    median age of gamers, 15

    metagames, 80–81, 84

INDEX

INDEX

INDEX

INDEX

INDEX

INDEX

ABOUT THE AUTHOR

Aaron Dignan dressed up like a superhero for the first 180 days of the first grade, which marked the beginning of his life as an iconoclast, observer, theorist, and performer. He is a founding partner of the digital strategy firm Undercurrent, based in New York, where he advises top executives at global brands like General Electric, PepsiCo, and Ford Motor Company helping them define their future in an increasingly technophilic world. Aaron's work at Undercurrent has been featured in *The New York Times, The Wall Street Journal, Forbes, Vanity Fair, Slate,* and *AdAge*.

Printed in the United States
By Bookmasters